ITF Taekwondo

Basic Information and Korean
for Belt Gradings

Keith McMullen

Introduction

This handbook presents a broad overview of the ITF Taekwon-do syllabus, a step-by-step guide through the patterns, theory, Korean words and hidden meanings of Taekwon-do thinking and power for easy reference and study. The book is designed to assist students from the beginning of their Taekwon-do journey, across their training and with all their belt gradings up to Black Belt.

The information has been drawn from my association and therefore it's possible some phrasing and spelling may differ from yours. If so, please consult your instructor for further clarification.

Happy Taekwon-do.

Keith McMullen.
Port Macquarie.

INDEX

ITF (International Taekwon-Do Federation)

A. FOUNDER of ITF TAEKWON-DO:

General Choi Hong Hi 9th Dan. 9th September 1918 – 15th May 2002.

B. DEFINITION of TAEKWON-DO (A KOREAN MARTIAL ART)

Tae means foot, or to strike with the feet. Kwon means hand, or to strike with the hand. Do means discipline, art, or way. Hence Taekwon-Do (foot-hand-way) literally means the art of the feet and the hands or the art of kicking and punching.

C. TAEKWON-DO TENETS

1. Courtesy **(Ye Ui)**
2. Integrity **(Yom Chi)**
3. Perseverance **(In Nae)**
4. Self-Control **(Guk Gi)**
5. Indomitable Spirit **(Baekjul Boolgool)**

D. TAEKWON-DO OATH

I shall observe the tenets of Taekwon-Do.
I shall respect the instructor and seniors.
I shall never misuse Taekwon-Do.
I shall be a champion of freedom and justice.
I shall build a more peaceful world.

E. NAMES, ORDER and BELTS of PATTERNS (TULS)

There are 2 exercises and 24 patterns due to the founder General Choi Hong Hi comparing the life of a man to a day in the life of the earth, and believing Taekwon-Do to be a legacy for coming generations.

For the sake of this handbook only the two exercises and the first 9 patterns leading up to black belt are addressed.

SAJU-JIRUGI (Exercise) - White belt, yellow tip
SAJU-MAKGI (Exercise) - White belt, yellow tip

Patterns:
1. **CHON-JI** - Yellow belt
2. **DAN-GUN** - Yellow belt, green tip
3. **DO-SAN** - Green belt
4. **WON-HYO** - Green belt, blue tip
5. **YUL-GOK** - Blue belt
6. **JOONG-GUN** - Blue belt, red tip
7. **TOI-GYE** - Red belt
8. **HWA-RANG** - Red belt, black tip
9. **CHOONG-MOO** - Black belt

F. SIGNIFICANCE of BELT COLOURS and (STRIPES)

The belts in Taekwon-Do symbolize ranking, with the white belt being the lowest and black the highest. In Taekwon-Do the student is graded for each new belt (or stripe) by performing the different moves of the pattern (Tul) that the student is currently studying. Each grading is to show mastery of the pattern with each pattern building the TKD skills sequentially on the previous one as the student progresses towards the black belt. If the instructor deems the student to have passed, the student will be rewarded with the next highest belt (or stripe).

White Belt:

White signifies the innocence as that of a beginning student who has no previous knowledge of Taekwon-Do.

Yellow Belt:
Yellow signifies the earth, from which the plant sprouts and takes root as the Taekwon-Do foundation is being laid.

Green Belt:
Green signifies the plant's growth as the Taekwon-Do skill begins to develop.

Blue Belt:
Blue signifies the heavens toward which the plant matures into a towering tree as the Taekwon-Do training progresses.

Red Belt:
Red signifies danger, cautioning the student to exercise control and warning the opponent to stay away.

Black Belt:
Black is the opposite of white, the beginner's colour, and therefore signifies maturity and proficiency in Taekwon-Do. It also indicates the wearer's imperviousness to darkness and fear.

G. INTERPRETATION OF EXERCISES and PATTERNS

SAJU JIRUGI   Four direction punch

SAJU-MAKGI   Four direction block

CHON-JI
Interpretation: Literal meaning of Chon-Ji is The Heaven and the Earth. It is, in the Orient, interpreted as the creation of the world or the beginning of human history, therefore it is the initial pattern played by the beginner. This pattern consists of two similar parts, one to represent the Heaven and the other the Earth.

DAN-GUN

Interpretation: Dan-Gun is named after the holy Dan Gun, the legendary founder of Korea in 2333 BC.

DO-SAN

Interpretation: Do-San is the pseudonym of the patriot Ahn Chang-Ho (1876-1938). The 24 movements represent his entire life which he devoted to furthering the education of Korea and its independence movement.

WON-HYO

Interpretation: Won-Hyo was the noted monk who introduced Buddhism to the Silla Dynasty in the year of 686 A.D.

YUL-GOK

Interpretation: Yul-Gok is the pseudonym of the great philosopher and scholar Yi 1 (1536-1584) nicknamed the 'Confucius of Korea'. The 38 movements of this pattern refer to his birthplace on the 38 latitude and the diagram represents 'scholar'.

JOONG-GUN

Interpretation: Joong-Gun is named after the patriot Ahn Joong-Gun who assassinated Hiro-Bumi Ito, the first Japanese governor-general of Korea, known as the man who played the leading part in the Korea-Japan merger. There are 32 movements in this pattern to represent Mr. Ahn's age when he was executed in a Lui-Shung prison (1910).

TOI-GYE

Interpretation: Toi-Gye is the pen name of the noted scholar Yi Hwang (16th century), an authority on neo-Confucianism. The 37 movements of the pattern refer to his birthplace on the 37th degree latitude, the diagram represents 'scholar'.

HWA-RANG

Interpretation: Hwa-rang is named after the Hwa-Rang youth group, which originated in the Silla Dynasty in the early 7th century. The 29 movements refer to the 29th Infantry Division, where Taekwon-Do developed into maturity.

CHOONG-MO
Interpretation: Choong-Mo was the name given to the great Admiral Yi Soon-Sin of the Lee Dynasty. He was reputed to have invented the first armoured battleship (Kobukson) in 1592, which is said to be the precursor of the present day submarine. The reason why this pattern ends with a left hand attack is to symbolize his regrettable death, having no chance to show his unrestrained potentiality checked by the forced reservation of his loyalty to the king.

H. THE NUMBER OF MOVEMENTS PER PATTERNS, STARTS and FINISHES.

SAJU JIRUGI
14 movements
Start: Parallel ready stance

SAJU MAKGI
16 movements
Start: Parallel ready stance

1. CHON-JI
19 movements
Start: Parallel ready stance
Finish: Left foot moves back to starting position

2. DAN-GUN
21 movements
Start: Parallel ready stance
Finish: Left foot moves back to starting position

3. DO-SAN
24 movements

Start: Parallel ready stance
Finish: Right foot moves back to starting position

4. WON-HYO

28 movements
Start: Closed ready stance A
Finish: Right foot moves back to starting position

5. YUL-GOK

38 movements
Start: Parallel ready stance
Finish: Left foot moves back to starting position

6. JOONG-GUN

32 movements
Start: Closed ready stance B
Finish: Left foot moves back to starting position

7. TOI-GYE

37 movements
Start: Closed ready stance B
Finish: Right foot moves back to starting position

8. HWA-RANG

29 movements
Start: Closed ready stance C
Finish: Right foot moves back to starting position

9. CHOONG-MOO (Black belt)

30 movements
Start: Parallel ready stance
Finish: Left foot moves back to starting position

I. KI-HAPS IN PATTERNS

The short shouts made before, during, or after a pattern are called Ki-haps. A Ki-hap is an energetic yell.

Chon-Ji: 1 Ki-hap, Movement #17 2nd forward front punch.

Dan-Gun: 2 Ki-haps, Movement #8 high punch before twin forearm block - and **Movement #17** last rising block.

Do-San: 2 Ki-haps, Movement #6 straight fingertip thrust - and **Movement #22** last rising block.

Won-Hyo: 1 Ki-hap, **Movement #12** straight fingertip thrust.

Yul-Gok: 3 Ki-haps, **Movements #24 & #27** both front elbow strikes - and movement **#36** jumping back-fist.

Joong-Gun: 1 Ki-hap, **Movement #12** twin upset punch.

Toi-Gye: 1 Ki-hap, Movement #29 jumping X-fist pressing block.

Hwa-Rang: 2 Ki-haps, **Movement #14** last walking stance middle section punch before spin knife-hand guarding block - and **Movement #25** right side elbow thrust.

Choong-Moo: 2 Ki-haps, **Movement #9** on the execution of the knife hand guarding block when landing from flying side kick - and **Movement #19** on the landing knife hand guarding block from the jump spin technique.

J. KOREAN TERMS PER PATTERNS and EXERCISES

NOTE: A) SAJU JIRUGI and B) SAJU MAKGI are exercises and NOT patterns. They are given to students to help develop co-ordination, direction change and breathing control.

1. SAJU JIRUGI (Four Directional punch) - White belt/Yellow tip

Step	Stance	Technique - Korean & English
1	R Gunnun (Walking)	**Kaunde baro ap jurugi** (Mid section obverse punch)
2	L Gunnun	**Najunde baro bakat palmok makgi** (Low section obverse outer forearm block**)**
3	R Gunnun	**Kaunde baro ap jurugi** (Mid section obverse punch)
4	L Gunnun	**Najunde baro bakat palmok makgi** (Low section obverse outer forearm block)
5	R Gunnun	**Kaunde baro ap jurugi** (Mid section obverse punch)
6	L Gunnun	**Najunde baro bakat palmok makgi** (Low section obverse outer forearm block)
7	R Gunnun	**Kaunde baro ap jurugi** (Mid section obverse punch)
8	Parallel ready	
9	L Gunnun	**Kaunde baro ap jurugi** (Mid section obverse punch)
10	R Gunnun	**Najunde baro bakat palmok makgi** (Low section obverse outer forearm block)
11	L Gunnun	**Kaunde baro ap jurugi** (Mid section obverse punch)
12	R Gunnun	**Najunde baro bakat palmok makgi** (Low section obverse outer forearm block)
13	L Gunnun	**Kaunde baro ap jurugi** (Mid section obverse punch)
14	R Gunnun	**Najunde baro bakat palmok makgi** (Low section obverse outer forearm block)

15	L Gunnun	**Kaunde baro ap jurugi** (Mid section obverse punch)
16	Parallel ready	

2. SAJU MAKGI (Four directional block) - White belt/Yellow tip

Identical direction and stance to Saju Jirugi except use low section knife hand block (najunde sonkal makgi) and middle section forearm block (kaunde an palmok makgi).

CHON-JI 9th Grade – Yellow Belt

Step	Stance	Technique - Korean & English
1	L Gunnun (Walking)	**Najunde bakat palmok makgi** (Low outer forearm block)
2	R Gunnun	**Kaunde baro ap jirugi** (Middle obverse punch)
3	R Gunnun	**Najunde bakat palmok makgi** (Low section outer forearm block)
4	L Gunnun	**Kaunde baro ap jirugi** (Middle section obverse punch)
5	L Gunnun	**Najunde bakat palmok makgi** (Low section outer forearm block)
6	R Gunnun	**Kaunde baro ap jirugi** (Middle section obverse punch)
7	R Gunnun	**Najunde bakat palmok makgi** (Low section outer forearm block)
8	L Gunnun	**Kaunde baro ap jirugi** (Middle section obverse punch)
9	R Niunja (L-stance)	**Kaunde an palmok makgi** (Middle section inner forearm block)

10	R Gunnun	**Kaunde baro ap jirugi** (Middle section obverse punch)
11	L Niunja	**Kaunde an palmok makgi** (Middle section inner forearm block)
12	L Gunnun	**Kaunde baro ap jirugi** (Middle section obverse punch)
13	R Niunja	**Kaunde an palmok makgi** (Middle section inner forearm block)
14	R Gunnun	**Kaunde baro ap jirugi** (Middle section obverse punch)
15	L Niunja	**Kaunde an palmok makgi** (Middle section inner forearm block)
16	L Gunnun	**Kaunde baro ap jirugi** (Middle section obverse punch)
17	R Gunnun	**Kaunde baro ap jirugi** (Middle section obverse punch) **KI-HAP!**
18	L Gunnun	**Kaunde baro ap jirugi** (Middle section obverse punch)
19	R Gunnun	**Kaunde baro ap jirugi** (Middle section obverse punch) **KI-HAP ... CHON-JI!**

DAN-GUN 8th Grade - Yellow Belt/Green Tip

Step	Stance	Technique - Korean & English
1	R Niunja	**Kaunde sonkal daebi makgi** (Middle section knife hand guarding block)
2	R Gunnun	**Nopunde baro ap jirugi** (High section obverse punch)
3	L Niunja	**Kaunde sonkal daebi makgi** (Middle section knife hand guarding block)
4	L Gunnun	**Nopunde baro ap jirugi** (High section obverse punch)

5	L Gunnun	**Najunde bakat palmok makgi** (Low section outer forearm block)
6	R Gunnun	**Nopunde baro ap jirugi** (High section obverse punch)
7	L Gunnun	**Nopunde baro ap jirugi** (High section obverse punch)
8	R Gunnun	**Nopunde baro ap jirugi** (High section obverse punch) **KI-HAP!**
9	R Niunja	**Sang palmok makgi** (Twin forearm block)
10	R Gunnun	**Nopunde baro ap jirugi** (High section obverse punch)
11	L Niunja	**Sang palmok makgi** (Twin forearm block)
12	L Gunnun	**Nopunde baro ap jirugi** (High section obverse punch)
13	L Gunnun	**Najunde bakat palmok makgi** (Low section outer forearm block)
14	L Gunnun	**Bakat palmok chookyo makgi** (Outer forearm rising block)
15	R Gunnun	**Bakat palmok chookyo makgi** (Outer forearm rising block)
16	L Gunnun	**Bakat palmok chookyo makgi** (Outer forearm rising block)
17	R Gunnun	**Bakat palmok chookyo makgi** (Outer forearm rising block) **KI-HAP!**
18	R Niunja	**Kaunde sonkal yop taerigi** (Middle section knife hand side strike)
19	R Gunnun	**Nopunde baro ap jirugi** (High section obverse punch)
20	L Niunja	**Kaunde sonkal yop taerigi** (Middle section knife hand side strike)
21	L Gunnun	**Nopunde baro ap jirugi** (High section obverse punch) **KI-HAP ... DAN-GUN!**

DO-SAN 7th Grade - Green Belt

Step	Stance	Technique - Korean & English
1	L Gunnun	**Nopunde bakat palmok yop makgi** (High section outer forearm side block)
2	L Gunnun	**Kaunde bandae jirugi** (Middle section reverse punch)
3	R Gunnun	**Nopunde bakat palmok yop makgi** (High section outer forearm side block)
4	R Gunnun	**Kaunde bandae jirugi** (Middle section reverse punch)
5	R Niunja	**Kaunde sonkal daebi makgi** (Middle section knife hand guarding block)
6	R Gunnun	**Kaunde son sonkut tulgi** (Middle section straight fingertip thrust) **KI-HAP!**
7	L Gunnun	**Nopunde dung joomuk yop taerigi** (High section back fist side strike)
8	R Gunnun	**Nopunde dung joomuk yop taerigi** (High section back fist side strike)
9	L Gunnun	**Nopunde bakat palmok yop makgi** (High section outer forearm block)
10	L Gunnun	**Kaunde bandae jirugi** (Middle section reverse punch)
11	R Gunnun	**Nopunde bakat palmok yop makgi** (High section outer forearm side block)
12	R Gunnun	**Kaunde bandae jirugi** (Middle section reverse punch)
13	L Gunnun	**Nopunde bakat palmok hechyo makgi** (High section outer forearm wedging block)
14	-	**Kaunde apcha busigi** (Middle section front snap kick)
15	R Gunnun	**Kaunde baro ap jirugi** (Middle section obverse punch)

16	R Gunnun	**Kaunde bandae ap jirugi** (Middle section reverse punch)
17	R Gunnun	**Nopunde bakat palmok hechyo makgi** (High section outer forearm wedging block)
18	-	**Kaunde apcha busigi** (Middle section front snap kick)
19	L Gunnun	**Kaunde baro ap jirugi** (Middle section obverse punch)
20	L Gunnun	**Kaunde bandae ap jirugi** (Middle section reverse punch)
21	L Gunnun	**Bakat palmok chookyo makgi** (Outer forearm rising block)
22	R Gunnun	**Bakat palmok chookyo makgi** (Outer forearm rising block) **KI-HAP!**
23	Annun (Sitting)	**Kaunde so sonkal yop taerigi** (Middle section knife hand side strike)
24	Annun	**Kaunde so sonkal yop taerigi** (Middle section knife hand side strike) **KI-HAP ... DO-SAN!**

WON-HYO 6th Grade - Green Belt/Blue Tip

Step	Stance	Technique - Korean & English
1	R Niunja (L Stance)	**Sang palmok makgi** (Twin forearm block)
2	R Niunja	**Nopunde anuro sonkal taerigi** (High section inward knife hand strike)
3	L Gojong (Fixed)	**Kaunde yop jirugi** (Middle section side punch)
4	R Niunja	**Sang palmok makgi** (Twin forearm block)
5	L Niunja	**Nopunde anuro sonkal taerigi** (High section inward knife hand strike)

6	R Gojong (Fixed)	**Kaunde yop jirugi** (Middle section side punch)
7	R Goburyo (Bending ready)	**Palmok daebi makgi** (Forearm guarding block)
8	-	**Kauede wen yopcha jirugi** (Middle section side kick and punch)
9	R Niunja	**Kauede sonkal daebi makgi** (Middle section knife hand guarding block)
10	L Niunja	**Kauede sonkal daebi makgi** (Middle section knife hand guarding block)
11	R Niunja	**Kauede sonkal daebi makgi** (Middle section knife hand guarding block)
12	R Gunnun	**Kaunde son sonkut tulgi** (Middle section fingertip thrust) **KI-HAP!**
13	R Niunja	**Sang palmok makgi** (Twin forearm block)
14	R Niunja	**Nopunde anuro sonkal taerigi** (High section inward knife hand strike)
15	L Gojong	**Kaunde yop jirugi** (Middle section side punch)
16	R Niunja	**Sang palmok makgi** (Twin forearm block)
17	L Niunja	**Nopunde anuro sonkal taerigi** (High section inward knife hand strike)
18	R Gojong	**Kaunde yop jirugi** (Middle section side punch)
19	L Gunnun	**Kaunde an palmok dollimyo makgi** (Middle section inner forearm circular block)
20	-	**Najunde apcha busigi** (Low section front snap kick)
21	R Gunnun	**Kaunde bandae ap jirugi** (Middle section reverse punch)
22	R Gunnun	**Kaunde an palmok dollimyo makgi** (Middle

		section inner forearm circular block)
23	-	**Najunde apcha busigi** (Low section front snap kick)
24	L Gunnun	**Kaunde bandae ap jirugi** (Middle section reverse punch)
25	L Guburyo	**Palmok daebi makgi** (Forearm guarding block)
26	-	**Kaunde orun yopcha jirugi** (Middle section right side kick)
27	R Niunja	**Kaunde palmok daebi makgi** (Middle section forearm guarding block)
28	L Niunja	**Kaunde palmok daebi makgi** (Middle section forearm guarding block) **KI-HAP ... WON-HYO!**

YUL-GOK 5th Grade - Blue Belt

Step	Stance	Technique - Korean & English
1	Annun (Sitting)	**Chojum jirugi** (Focus punch – left fist)
2	Annun	**Kaunde ap jirugi** (R) (Middle section punch)
3	Annun	**Kaunde ap jirugi** (L) (Middle section punch)
4	Annun	**Chojum jirugi** (Focus punch - right fist)
5	Annun	**Kaunde ap jirugi** (L) (Middle section punch)
6	Annun	**Kaunde ap jirugi** (R) (Middle section punch)
7	R Gunnun	**Kaunde an palmok makgi** (Middle section inner forearm block)
8	-	**Najunde apcha busigi** (Lower section front snap kick)
9	L Gunnun	**Kaunde baro ap jirugi** (Middle section obverse punch)
10	L Gunnun	**Kaunde bandae ap jirugi** (Middle section reverse punch)

11	L Gunnun	**Kaunde an palmok makgi** (Middle section inner forearm block)
12	-	**Najunde apcha busigi** (Lower section front snap kick)
13	R Gunnun	**Kaunde baro ap jirugi** (Middle section obverse punch)
14	R Gunnun	**Kaunde bandae ap jirugi** (Middle section reverse punch)
15	R Gunnun	**Kaunde golcho makgi** (Middle section hooking block)
16	R Gunnun	**Kaunde bandae golcho makgi** (Middle section reverse hooking block)
17	R Gunnun	**Kaunde baro ap jirugi** (Middle section obverse punch)
18	L Gunnun	**Kaunde golcho makgi** (Middle section hooking block)
19	L Gunnun	**Kaunde bandae golcho makgi** (Middle section reverse hooking block)
20	L Gunnun	**Kaunde baro ap jirugi** (Middle section obverse punch)
21	R Gunnun	**Kaunde baro ap jirugi** (Middle section obverse punch)
22	R Guburyo (Bending ready stance)	
23	-	**Kaunde yopcha jirugi** (Middle section side piercing kick)
24	L Gunnun	**Kaunde ap palkup taerigi** (Middle section front elbow strike) **KI-HAP!**
25	L Goburyo (Bending ready stance)	
26	-	**Kaunde yopcha jirugi** (Middle section side

		piercing kick)
27	R Gunnun	**Kaunde ap palkup taerigi** (Middle section front elbow strike) **KI-HAP!**
28	R Niunja	**Sang sonkal makgi** (Twin knife hand block)
29	R Gunnun	**Kaunde son sonkut tulgi** (Middle section straight fingertip thrust)
30	L Niunja	**Sang sonkal makgi** (Twin knife hand block)
31	L Gunnun	**Kaunde son sonkut tulgi** (Middle section straight fingertip thrust)
32	L Gunnun	**Nopunde bakat palmok yop makgi** (High section outer forearm side block)
33	L Gunnun	**Kaunde bandae jirugi** (Middle section reverse punch)
34	R Gunnun	**Nopunde bakat palmok yop makgi** (High section outer forearm side block)
35	R Gunnun	**Kaunde bandae ap jirugi** (Middle section reverse punch)
36	L Kyocha (x-stance)	**Nopunde dung joomuk yop taerigi** (High section back fist side strike) **KI-HAP!**
37	R Gunnun	**Nopunde doo palmok makgi** (High section double forearm block)
38	L Gunnun	**Nopunde doo palmok makgi** (High section double forearm block) **KI-HAP ... YUL-GOK!**

JOONG-GUN 4th Grade - Blue Belt/Red Tip

Step	Stance	Technique - Korean & English
1	R Niunja	**Kaunde sonkal dung yop makgi** (Middle section reverse knife hand side block)
2	-	**Najunde apcha busigi** (Lower section front snap kick)

3	L Dwitbal (Rear foot)	**Kaunde ollyo sonbadak makgi** (Middle section upwards palm block)
4	L Niunja	**Kaunde sonkal dung yop makgi** (Middle section reverse knife hand side block)
5	-	**Najunde apcha busigi** (Lower section front snap kick)
6	R Dwitbal (Rear foot)	**Kaunde ollyo son badak makgi** (Middle section upwards palm block)
7	L Niunja	**Kaunde sonkal daebi makgi** (Middle section knife hand guarding block)
8	L Gunnun	**Wi palkup taerigi** (Upper elbow strike)
9	L Niunja	**Kaunde sonkal daebi makgi** (Middle section knife hand guarding block)
10	R Gunnun	**Wi palkup taerigi** (Upper elbow strike)
11	L Gunnun	**Nopunde sang sewo jirugi** (Upper section twin vertical punch)
12	R Gunnun	**Sang dwijibo jirugi** (Twin upset punch) **KI-HAP!**
13	L Gunnun	**Kyocha chookyo makgi** (X-fist rising block)
14	R Niunja	**Nopunde dung joomuk yop taerigi** (Upper section back fist side strike)
15	L Gunnun	Release move
16	L Gunnun	**Nopunde bandae jirugi** (High section reverse punch)
17	L Niunja	**Nopunde dung joomuk yop taerigi** (Upper section back fist side strike)
18	R Gunnun	Release move
19	R Gunnun	**Nopunde bandae jirugi** (High section reverse punch)
20	L Gunnun	**Nopunde doo palmok makgi** (Upper section double forearm block)

21	R Niunja	**Kaunde yop jirugi** (Middle section side punch)
22	-	**Kaunde yopcha jirugi** (Middle section side piercing kick)
23	R Gunnun	**Nopunde doo palmok makgi** (Upper section double forearm block)
24	L Niunja	**Kaunde yop jirugi** (Middle section side punch)
25	-	**Kaunde yopcha jirugi** (Middle section side piercing kick)
26	R Niunja	**Kaunde palmok daebi makgi** (Middle section forearm guarding block)
27	L Nachuo (Low)	**Sonbadak noollo makgi** (Palm pressing block)
28	L Niunja	**Kaunde palmok daebi makgi** (Middle section forearm guarding block)
29	R Nachuo (Low)	**Sonbadak noollo makgi** (Palm pressing block)
30	Moa (Close)	**Kaunde dollyo jirugi** (Middle section turning punch - slow)
31	R Gojung (Fixed)	**Digutja makgi** (U-shaped block)
32	L Gojung (Fixed)	**Digutja makgi** (U-shaped block) **KI-HAP ... JOONG-GUN!**

TOI-GYE 3rd Grade - Red Belt

Step	Stance	Technique - Korean & English
1	R Niunja	**Kaunde an palmok makgi** (Middle section inner forearm block)
2	L Gunnun	**Najunde dwijibo sonkut tulgi** (Low section upset fingertip thrust)

3	Moa (Close)	**Najunde bakat palmok makgi** (Low section outer forearm block) & **Nopunde dung joomuk yop taerigi** (slow) (High section back fist side back strike)
4	L Niunja	**Kaunde an palmok makgi** (Middle section inner forearm block)
5	R Gunnun	**Najunde dwijibo sonkut tulgi** (Low section upset fingertip thrust)
6	Moa (Close)	**Najunde bakat palmok makgi** (Low section outer forearm block) & **Nopunde dung joomuk yop taerigi** (slow) (High section back fist side back strike) as move 3 (opposite hands)
7	L Gunnun	**Najunde noollo kyocha makgi** (Low section downwards X-fist pressing block)
8	L Gunnun	**Nopunde sang sewo jirugi** (High section twin vertical punch)
9	-	**Kaunde apcha busigi** (Middle section front snap kick)
10	R Gunnun	**Kaunde baro ap jirugi** (Middle section obverse punch)
11	R Gunnun	**Kaunde bandae ap jirugi** (Middle section reverse punch) 11 & 12 performed in a continuous motion.
12	Moa	**Sang yop palkup tulgi** (Twin side elbow thrust)
13	Annun	**Orun san makgi** (W shape block) looking right
14	Annun	**Wen san makgi** (W shape block) looking left
15	Annun	**Wen san makgi** (W shape block) looking left
16	Annun	**Orun san makgi** (W shape block) looking right
17	Annun	**Wen san makgi** (W shape block) looking left
18	Annun	**Wen san makgi** (W shape block) looking left
19	R Niunja	**Najunde doo palmok miro makgi** (Low section double forearm pushing block)

20	L Gunnun	**Mori jupke** (Head grasp)
21	-	**Ollyo moorup chagi** (Upward knee kick)
22	R Niunja	**Kaunde sonkal daebi makgi** (Middle knife hand guarding block)
23	-	**Najunde yop apcha busigi** (front leg) (Low section side front snap kick)
24	L Gunnun	**Nopunde opun sonkut tulgi** (High section flat fingertip thrust)
25	L Niunja	**Kaunde sonkal daebi makgi** (Middle knife hand guarding block)
26	-	**Najunde yop apcha busigi** (front leg) (Low section front side snap kick)
27	R Gunnun	**Nopunde opun sonkut tulgi** (High section flat fingertip thrust)
28	R Niunja	**Nopunde dung joomuk yopdwi taerigi** (High section back fist side back strike) & **Najunde bakat palmok makgi** (Low section outer forearm block)
29	R Kyocha (X-stance)	**Najunde kyocha joomuk noollo makgi** (Low section X-fist pressing block) **KI-HAP!**
30	R Gunnun	**Nopunde doo palmok makgi** (High section double forearm block)
31	R Niunja	**Najunde sonkal daebi makgi** (Low section knife hand guarding block)
32	L Gunnun	**Kaunde dollimyo an palmok makgi** (Middle section inner forearm circular block)
33	L Niunja	**Najunde sonkal daebi makgi** (Low section knife hand guarding block)
34	R Gunnun	**Kaunde dollimyo an palmok makgi** (Middle section inner forearm circular block)
35	L Gunnun	**Kaunde dollimyo an palmok makgi** (Middle section inner forearm circular block)

| 36 | R Gunnun | **Kaunde dollimyo an palmok makgi** (Middle section inner forearm circular block) |
| 37 | Annun | **Kaunde orun ap jirugi** (Middle section right punch) **KI-HAP ... TOI-GYE!** |

HWA-RANG 2nd Grade - Red Belt/Black Tip

Step	Stance	Technique - Korean & English
1	Annun	**Kaunde son badak miro makgi** (Middle section palm pushing block)
2	-	**Kaunde orun ap jirugi** (Middle section right front punch)
3	-	**Kaunde wen ap jirugi** (Middle section left front punch) (Fast motion) 2 & 3 performed in a continuous motion.
4	L Niunja	**Sang palmok makgi** (Twin forearm block)
5	-	**Ollyo wen jirugi** (Upwards left punch)
6	R Gojung (Fixed)	**Kaunde orun yop jirugi** (Middle section right front punch)
7	R Soojik	**Naeryo sonkal taerigi** (Downward hand strike)
8	L Gunnun	**Kaunde baro ap jirugi** (Middle section obverse front punch)
9	L Gunnun	**Najunde bakat palmok makgi** (Low section outer forearm block)
10	R Gunnun	**Kaunde baro ap jirugi** (Middle section obverse punch)
11		(Grasp right fist with left hand)
12	L Niunja	**Kaunde yopcha jirugi** (Middle section side piercing kick) **Kaunde sonkal yop taerigi** (Middle section knife hand side strike) Continuous motion.

13	L Gunnun	**Kaunde baro ap jirugi** (Middle section obverse punch)
14	R Gunnun	**Kaunde baro ap jirugi** (Middle section obverse punch) **KI-HAP!**
15	R Niunja	**Kaunde sonkal daebi makgi** (Middle section knife hand guarding block)
16	R Gunnun	**Kaunde son sonkut tulgi** (Middle section straight fingertip thrust)
17	R Niunja	**Kaunde sonkal daebi makgi** (Middle section knife hand guarding block)
18	-	**Nopunde dollyo chagi** (High section turning kick)
19	-	**Nopunde dollyo chagi** (High section turning kick) **Kaunde sonkal daebi makgi** (Middle section knife hand guarding block) 18 & 19 performed in a continuous motion.
20	L Gunnun	**Najunde bakat palmok makgi** (Low section outer forearm block)
21	R Niunja	**Kaunde baro ap jirugi** (Middle section obverse punch)
22	L Niunja	**Kaunde baro ap jirugi** (Middle section obverse punch)
23	R Niunja	**Kaunde baro ap jirugi** (Middle section obverse punch)
24	L Gunnun	**Najunde kyocha joomuk noollo makgi** (Low section X-fist pressing block)
25	R Niunja	**Yop palkup orun tulgi** (Side elbow right thrust) **KI-HAP!**
26	Moa	**Kaunde an palmok orun yop makgi** (Middle section inner forearm right side block) & **Najunde bakat palmok wen makgi** (Low section outer forearm left block)
27	-	(change position of hands)

| 28 | R Niunja | **Kaunde sonkal daebi makgi** (Middle section knife hand guarding block) |
| 29 | L Niunja | **Kaunde sonkal daebi makgi** (Middle section knife hand guarding block) **KI-HAP ... HWA-RANG!** |

CHOONG-MOO 1st Grade - Black Belt

Step	Stance	Technique - Korean & English
1	R Niunja	**Sang sonkal makgi** (Twin knife hand block)
2	R Gunnun	**Nopunde sonkal anuro taerigi** (High section knife hand inward strike)
3	L Niunja	**Kaunde sonkal daebi makgi** (Middle section knife hand guarding block)
4	L Gunnun	**Nopunde opun sonkut tulgi** (High section flat left fingertip thrust)
5	R Niunja	**Kaunde sonkal daebi makgi** (Middle section knife hand guarding block)
6	Guburyo (Bending)	
7	Narani junbi	**Kaunde yopcha jirugi** (Middle section side kick)
8	R Niunja	**Kaunde sonkal daebi makgi** (Middle section knife hand guarding block)
9	L Niunja	**Twimyo yopcha jirugi** (Flying side piercing kick) **Kaunde sonkal daebi makgi** (Middle section knife hand guarding block) **KI-HAP!**
10	R Niunja	**Najunde bakat palmok makgi** (Low section outer forearm block)
11	L Gunnun	**Mori jupke** (Head grasp)
12		**Moorup ollyo chagi** (Upward knee kick)
13	L Gunnun	**Nopunde sonkal dung ap taerigi** (High section reverse knife hand strike)

14		**Nopunde dollyo chagi** (High section turning kick)
15		**Kaunde dwitcha jirugi** (Middle section back piercing kick)
16	L Niunja	**Kaunde palmok daebi makgi** (Middle section forearm guarding block)
17		**Kaunde dollyo chagi** (Middle section turning kick)
18	Gojung (Fixed)	**Digutja makgi** (U-shaped block)
19	L Niunja	**Kaunde sonkal daebi makgi** (Middle section knife hand guarding block) **KI-HAP!**
20	L Gunnun	**Najunde dwijibun sonkut tulgi** (Low section upset fingertip thrust)
21	R Niunja	**Nopunde dung joomuk yop taerigi** (High section back fist back side strike) **najunde bakat palmok makgi** (Low section outer forearm block)
22	R Gunnun	**Kaunde sun sonkut tulgi** (Middle section straight fingertip thrust)
23	L Gunnun	**Nopunde doo palmok makgi** (High section double forearm block)
24	Annun (Sitting)	**Kaunde an palmok ap makgi** (Middle section inner forearm front block) **Nopunde dung joomuk yop taerigi** (High section back fist side strike)
25		**Kaunde yopcha jirugi** (Middle section side kick)
26		**Kaunde yopcha jirugi** (Middle section side kick)
27	L Niunja	**Kyocha sonkal momchau makgi** (X-knife hand checking block)
28	L Gunnun	**Sang sonbadak ollyo makgi** (Twin palm upward block)
29	R Gunnun	**Bakat palmok chookyo makgi** (Outer forearm rising block)
30	R Gunnun	**Kaunde bandae ap jirugi** (Middle section reverse punch) **KI-HAP ... CHOONG-MOO!**

K. COUNTING TO TEN IN KOREAN

1: **Hanah**
2: **Dool**
3: **Set**
4: **Net**
5: **Dasot**
6: **Yasot**
7: **Ilgop**
8: **Yadol**
9: **Ahop**
10: **Yool**

L. UNIFORM & MISCELLANEOUS

Uniform - **Dobok**
Belt - **Dhee**
Training hall - **Dojang**
Pattern - **Tul**
Student - **Jeja**
Instructor - **Sah-bum (Sabum)**
Assistant Instructor - Sun-bae min
Demonstration - **Sibum**
Sparring - **Matsogi**

M. COMMANDS

Attention - **Cha ryuht**
Bow - **Kyong ye**
Ready - **Choon bi**
Begin - **Si-jak**
Return to starting position - **Bah ro**
Stop - **Goman (also Mum cho)**
Turn - **Dorah**
At ease - **Swiyo**

Stand - **Elosoh**
Separate **- Hechyo**
Continue - **Kae sok**
Dismiss - **Hae san**
Face the flag - **Gooki-eh De-ha-yeo**
Face instructor/master and bow - **Sah-bum nim keh, kyong ye**
Face senior student and bow - **Boo Sun-bae nim keh, kyong ye**
Face examiner/tester - **Simsa-kwan nim keh**

N. TITLES

Instructor (or 'master') - **Sah-bum nim (Sabum)**
Senior student - **Sun-bae nim**
Junior student - **Hu-bae nim**

O. KOREAN TERMS

Punch - **Jirugi**
Kick - **Chagi**
Block - **Makgi**
Stance - **Sogi**
Strike - **Tearigi**
Thrust -**Tulgi**
Guarding - **Daebi**

P. DIRECTIONS

Turning - **Dollyo**
Upwards - **Ollyo**
Rising - **Chookyo**
Pressing - **Noollo**
Downwards - **Naeryo**
Inward - **Anaero**
Outward - **Bakaero**

Straight - **Sun**
Left - **Wen**
Right - **Orun**
Reverse - **Bandae**
Obverse - **Baro**
Flying - **Twimyo**
Jumping - **Twigi**
Vertical - **Soojik**

Q. SECTIONS OF THE BODY

High - **Nopunde**
Middle - **Kaunde**
Low - **Najunde**
Front - **Ap**
Side - **Yop**
Back - **Dwit (also dung)**

R. HAND PARTS

Fist - **Joomuk**
Fore fist - **Ap joomuk**
Back fist - **Dung joomuk**
Side fist - **Yop joomuk**
Open fist - **Pung joomuk**
Hand/palm - **Son**
Palm - **Sonbadak**
Knife hand - **Sonkal**
Backhand - **Sondung**
Fingers - **Sun/son**
Fingertip - **Sunkut**

S. FOOT PARTS

Ball of foot - **Apkumchi**
Foot sword - **Bakal**
Instep - **Baltung**
Toes - **Balkut**
Heel - **Dwichook**
Knee - **Moorup**

T. PARTS OF THE BODY

Forearm - **Palmok**
Inner forearm - **An palmok**
Outer forearm - **Bakat palmok**
Elbow - **Palkup**
Arm - **Pal**
Head - **Mori**

U. BASIC BLOCKS, STANCES, PUNCHES, KICKS, THRUSTS and STRIKES

1) Blocks - Makgi

Low block - **Najunde palmok makgi**
Inner forearm block - **An palmok makgi**
Outer forearm block - **Bakat palmok makgi**
Guarding block - **Daebi makgi**
Knifehand guarding block - **Sonkal daebi makgi**
Twin knifehand block - **Sang sonkal makgi**
Double forearm block - **Doo palmok makgi**
Twin forearm block - **Sang palmok makgi**
Rising block - **Chookyo makgi**
Upward block - **Sonbadak olloyo makgi**
Circular block - **Dollimyo makgi**
Hooking block - **Glocho makgi**

X-fist block - **Kyocha joomuk makgi**
X-knife hand checking block - **Kyocha sonkal momchau makgi**
Pressing block - **Noollo makgi**
Wedging block - **Hechyo makgi**
U-shaped block - **Digutja makgi**
W-shaped block - **San makgi**

2) Stances - Sogi

Attention stance - **Charyot sogi**
Parallel Ready stance - **Narani junbi sogi**
Walking stance - **Gunnun sogi**
L stance - **Niunja sogi**
Sitting stance - **Annun sogi**
Close stance - **Moa sogi**
Close ready stance - **Moa junbi sogi**
Fixed stance - **Gojung sogi**
Low stance - **Nachuo sogi**
Bending stance - **Guburyo sogi**
X-stance - **Kyocha sogi**
Vertical stance - **Soojik sogi**

3) Punches - Jirugi

Obverse punch - **Baro jirugi**
Reverse punch - **Bandae jirugi**
Side punch - **Yop jirugi**
Upward punch - **Ollyo jirugi**
Twin upset punch - **Sang dwijibo jirugi**
Twin vertical punch - **Sang sewo jurugi**

4) Kicks - Chagi

Front kick - **Ap chagi**
Side kick - **Yop chagi**
Turning kick - **Dollyo chagi**
Front snap kick - **Apcha bisugi**
Side piercing kick - **Yopcha jirugi**
Back piercing kick - **Dwitcha jirugi**

Flying side piercing kick - **Twimyo yopcha jirugi**
Downward kick - **Naeryo chagi**
Reverse turning kick - **Bandae dollyo chagi**
Reverse hooking kick - **Bandae goro chagi**
Hooking kick - **Glocha chagi**

5) Thrust - Tulgi

Straight fingertip thrust - **Sun sunkut tulgi**
Flat fingertip thrust - **Opun sunkut tulgi**

6) Strike - Taerigi

Elbow strike - **Palkup taerigi**
Upper elbow strike - **Wi palkup taerigi**
Knifehand strike - **Sonkal taerigi**
Reverse knifehand - **Sonkal dung taerigi**
Side strike **Yop taerigi**
Backfist strike - **Dung joomuk taerigi**
Backfist side strike - **Dung joomuk yop taerigi**
Front backfist strike - **Ap dung joomuk taerigi**
Knife hand downward strike - **Sonkal naeryo tearigi**

V. ALL TULS PICTURED, STEP B Y STEP.

THE FIRST FUNDAMENTAL MOVEMENT

SAJU JIRUGI

(White belt)

Saju Jirugi means Four Direction Punch. The student rotates counterclockwise pivoting on the left foot and performs four right-handed punches in different directions as the student pivots in a complete circle. The moves are then repeated rotating clockwise pivoting on the right foot with four left-handed punches.

1. SAJU JIRUGI. Parallel ready stance. **Narani junbi sogi.**

2. SAJU JIRUGI. Preparing to punch.

3. SAJU JIRUGI. First directional punch. Walking stance, middle section obverse punch. **Kaunde baro ap jurugi.**

4. SAJU JIRUGI. Right foot half back, pivot 90 degrees on left foot for low section block.

5. <u>SAJU JIRUGI</u>. Walking stance, outer forearm low section block.
Gunnun sogi, bakat palmok najunde makgi.

6. <u>SAJU JIRUGI</u>. Preparing for second directional punch.

7. <u>SAJU JIRUGI</u>. Second punch after turning 90 degrees. Walking stance, middle section punch. **Gunnun sogi, kaunde ap jirugi.**

8. <u>SAJU JIRUGI</u>. Pivot 90 degrees on left foot and block. Walking stance, outer forearm low section block. **Gunnun sogi, bakat palmok najunde makgi.**

9. <u>SAJU JIRUGI</u>. Third directional punch. Walking stance, middle section punch. **Gunnun sogi, kaunde ap jirugi.**

10. <u>SAJU JIRUGI</u>. Pivot 90 degrees on left foot and block. Walking stance, outer forearm low section block. **Gunnun sogi, bakat palmok najunde makgi.**

11. <u>SAJU JIRUGI</u>. Fourth directional punch. Walking stance, middle section punch. **Gunnun sogi, kaunde ap jirugi.**

12. <u>SAJU JIRUGI</u>. Return right leg to ready stance. **Narani junbi sogi.**

13. <u>SAJU JIRUGI</u>. Saju Jirugi is now repeated in the clockwise direction pivoting on the right foot with four left-handed punches as the student rotates. To finish ... left walking stance, middle section obverse punch. **Gunnun sogi, kaunde ap jirugi. Then shout KIHAP! and SAJU JIRUGI,**

14. <u>SAJU JIRUGI</u>. Bring left leg back to parallel ready stance. **Narani junbi sogi.** The student has now turned a complete circle with four punches in each direction.

THE SECOND FUNDAMENTAL MOVEMENT

SAJU MAKGI

(White belt with a yellow stripe)

Saju Makgi means Four Direction Block. The student rotates counterclockwise pivoting on the left foot starting with four left-handed knife hand low section blocks in four different directions as the student pivots in a complete circle. The moves are then repeated rotating clockwise pivoting on the right foot and starting with four right-handed blocks.

1. SAJU MAKGI. Parallel ready stance. **Narani junbi sogi.**

2. SAJU MAKGI. Preparing to block.

3. <u>SAJU MAKGI</u>. Right foot back into left walking stance with knife hand low section block. **Gunnun sogi, sonkal najunde makgi.**

4. <u>SAJU MAKGI</u>. Right foot forward, preparing to block.

5. <u>SAJU MAKGI</u>. Walking stance, inner forearm middle section block.
Gunnun sogi, an palmok kaunde makgi.

6. <u>SAJU MAKGI</u>. Right foot half back to pivot on the left foot 90 degrees,
preparing to block.

7. <u>SAJU MAKGI</u>. Walking stance, block with left knife hand low section block. **Gunnun sogi, sonkal najunde makgi.**

8. <u>SAJU MAKGI</u>. Walking stance, inner forearm middle section block. **Gunnun sogi, an palmok kaunde makgi.**

9. <u>SAJU MAKGI</u>. Right foot back to pivot 90 degrees to the left. Walking stance, block with left knife hand low section block. **Gunnun sogi, sonkal najunde makgi.**

10. <u>SAJU MAKGI</u>. Walking stance, inner forearm middle section block. **Gunnun sogi, an palmok kaunde makgi.**

11. <u>SAJU MAKGI</u>. Right foot back to pivot 90 degrees to the left on the left foot. Walking stance, block with left knife hand low section block.
Gunnun sogi, sonkal najunde makgi.

12. <u>SAJU MAKGI</u>. Walking stance, inner forearm middle section block.
Gunnun sogi, an palmok kaunde makgi.

13. <u>SAJU MAKGI</u>. Right leg returns to parallel ready stance. **Narani junbi sogi.**

14. <u>SAJU MAKGI</u>. Saju Makgi is now repeated in the clockwise direction pivoting on the right foot with four left-handed blocks as the student rotates. To finish ... left walking stance, inner forearm block. **Gunnun sogi, ap palmok kaunde kaunde makgi** and shout **KIHAP!** and **SAJU MAKGI**.

15. <u>SAJU MAKGI</u>. Step back into parallel ready stance. **Narani junbi sogi.** The student has now turned a complete circle with four blocks in each direction.

CHON-JI

(Yellow belt)

The literal meaning of Chon-Ji is the Heaven and the Earth. This Tul (a taekwondo pattern or exercise) consists of two parts which are similar. One represents Heaven and the other the Earth. The creation of the world is interpreted, across the Orient, as the beginning of human history. And so, this Tul is for the taekwondo beginner.

1. **CHON-JI.** Parallel ready stance. **Narani junbi sogi.**

2. **CHON-JI.** Preparing to block.

3. **CHON-JI.** Turn 90% to the left into left walking stance, outer forearm low section block. **Gunnun sogi, bakat palmok najunde makgi.**

4. **CHON-JI.** Ready to punch.

5. **CHON-JI.** Right walking stance, middle section punch. **Gunnun sogi, kaunde ap jirugi.**

6. **CHON-JI.** Starting to turn 180 degrees.

7. **CHON-JI.** Having turned right, now ready to block.

8. **CHON-JI.** Turn is complete with right walking stance, forearm low section block. **Gunnun sogi, bakat palmok najunde makgi.**

9. **<u>CHON-JI.</u>** Step into left walking stance, middle section block. **Gunnun sogi, kaunde ap jirugi.**

10. **<u>CHON-JI.</u>** Preparing to block an attack from the left.

11. **CHON-JI.** Turn 90 degrees to the left into left walking stance, outer forearm low section block. **Gunnun sogi, bakat palmok najunde makgi.**

12. **CHON-JI.** Stepping forward into right walking stance, middle section punch. **Gunnun sogi kaunde ap jirugi.**

13. **CHON-JI.** Turn 180 degrees into right walking stance, outer forearm low section block. **Gunnun sogi, bakat palmok najunde makgi.**

14. **CHON-JI.** Forward step into left walking stance, middle section punch. **Gunnun sogi, kaunde ap jirugi.**

15. **CHON-JI.** Preparing for an attack from the left.

16. **CHON-JI.** Turning 90 degrees to the left into L-stance, inner forearm middle section block. **Niunja sogi, an palmok kaunde makgi.**

17. **CHON-JI.** Stepping into a right walking stance, middle section punch. **Gunnun sogi, kaunde ap jirugi.**

18. **CHON-JI.** Right turn 180 degrees into left L- stance, inner forearm middle section block. **Niunja sogi, an palmok kaunde makgi.**

19. **CHON-JI.** Step into a left walking stance, middle section punch. **Gunnun sogi, kaunde ap jirugi.**

20. **CHON-JI.** Tuning 90 degrees into right L-stance, inner forearm middle section block. **Niunja sogi, an palmok kaunde makgi.**

21. **CHON-JI.** Stepping forward into right walking stance, middle section punch. **Gunnun sogi, kaunde ap jirugi.**

22. **CHON-JI.** Step forward into left L-stance, inner forearm middle section block. **Niunja sogi, an palmok kaunde makgi.**

23. **CHON-JI.** Stepping forward into left walking stance, middle section punch. **Gunnun sogi, kaunde ap jirugi.**

24. **CHON-JI.** Stepping forward into right walking stance, middle section punch. **Gunnun sogi, kaunde ap jirugi.**

25. **CHON-JI.** Step backwards with right leg into left walking stance, middle section punch. **Gunnun sogi, kaunde ap jirugi.**

26. **CHON-JI.** Step backwards with left leg into right walking stance, middle section punch. **Gunnun sogi, kaunde ap jirugi. SHOUT KIHAP!** and **CHON-JI.**

27. **CHON-JI.** Finish by bringing the left foot forward in parallel ready stance. **Narani junbi sogi.**

DAN-GUN

(Yellow belt with green stripe)

Dan-Gun introduces new skills that build on the ITF taekwondo foundations of punching and blocking.

This tul is named after the holy Dan-Gun the legendary founder of Korea in the year 2333 BC.

1. **DAN-GUN.** Parallel ready stance. **Narani junbi sogi.**

2. **DAN-GUN.** Preparing to block an attack from the left with the right palm facing outwards and the left palm facing inwards.

3. <u>**DAN-GUN.**</u> Turn 90 degrees to the left into L-stance, with a knife hand middle section block. **Niunja sogi, sonkal kaunde daebi makgi.**

4. <u>**DAN-GUN.**</u> Prepare to punch.

5. **<u>DAN-GUN.</u>** Step forward into a right walking stance and a high section punch. **Gunnun sogi, nopunde ap jirugi.**

6. **<u>DAN-GUN.</u>** Turning 180 degrees to the right on the left foot with raised hands.

7. <u>DAN-GUN.</u> Once the turn is complete, left L-stance with a knife hand middle section block. **Niunja sogi, sonkal kaunde daebi makgi.**

8. <u>DAN-GUN.</u> Step forward into left walking stance with a high section punch. **Gunnun sogi, nopunde ap jirugi.**

9. <u>**DAN-GUN.**</u> Prepare to block an attack from the left with raised hands.

10. <u>**DAN-GUN.**</u> Turn 90 degrees on the left foot into left walking stance with an outer forearm low section block. **Gunnun sogi, bakat palmok najunde makgi.**

11. <u>DAN-GUN.</u> Step forward into right walking stance and a high section punch. **Gunnun sogi, nopunde ap jirugi.**

12. <u>DAN-GUN.</u> Step forward into left walking stance and a high section punch. **Gunnun sogi, nopunde ap jirugi.**

13. <u>DAN-GUN.</u> Step forward into right walking stance and a high section punch. **Gunnun sogi, nopunde ap jirugi. Shout KIHAP!**

14. <u>DAN-GUN.</u> Turn 270 degrees on the right foot to the left with raised hand, palms facing inwards and the right hand on the outer.

15. <u>DAN-GUN.</u> Left foot forward into L-stance, twin forearm block.
Niunja sogi, sang palmok magki.

16. <u>DAN-GUN.</u> Step forward into a right walking stance, high section
punch. **Gunnun sogi, nopunde ap jirugi.**

17. DAN-GUN. Prepare to turn 180 degrees to the right, both hands raised with palms facing inwards.

18. DAN-GUN. Right foot forward into L-stance, twin forearm block.
Niunja sogi, sang palmok magki.

19. <u>DAN-GUN.</u> Step forward into left walking stance, high section punch. **Gunnun sogi, nopunde ap jirugi.**

20. <u>DAN-GUN.</u> Turn 90 degrees on the left foot into left walking stance, outer forearm low section block. **Gunnun sogi, bakat palmok najunde makgi.**

21. DAN-GUN. Left walking stance, outer forearm rising block. **Gunnun sogi, bakat palmok chookyo makgi.**

22. DAN-GUN. Right walking stance, outer forearm rising block. **Gunnun sogi, bakat palmok chookyo makgi.**

23. <u>DAN-GUN.</u> Left walking stance, outer forearm rising block. **Gunnun sogi, bakat palmok chookyo makgi.**

24. <u>DAN-GUN.</u> Right walking stance, outer forearm rising block. **Gunnun sogi, bakat palmok chookyo makgi.**

25. <u>DAN-GUN.</u> Turn 270 degrees to the left, raised hands with the back of them touching.

26. <u>DAN-GUN.</u> Complete the turn into a right L-stance, knife hand side strike. **Niunja sogi, sonkal yop taerigi.**

27. <u>DAN-GUN.</u> Step forward into a right walking stance, high section punch. **Gunnun sogi, nopunde ap jirugi.**

28. <u>DAN-GUN.</u> Turn 180 degrees into a left L-stance, knife hand side strike. **Niunja sogi, sonkal yop taerigi.**

29. <u>DAN-GUN.</u> Step forward into a right walking stance, high section punch. **Gunnun sogi, nopunde ap jirugi. Shout KIHAP!** And then **DAN-GUN!**

30. <u>DAN-GUN.</u> Bring the left leg back into a parallel ready stance to complete the tul. **Narani junbi sogi.**

DO-SAN

(Green belt)

Do-San is the pseudonym of the patriot Ahn Chang-Ho (1876 – 1938). The twenty-four movements represent his entire life which he devoted to furthering education in Korea and to its independence movement.

1. **DO-SAN.** Parallel ready stance to prepare for the tul. **Narani junbi sogi.**

2. **DO-SAN.** Turn 180 degrees into left walking stance to block with outer forearm high section side block. **Gunnun sogi, bakat palmok nopunde yop makgi.**

3. **<u>DO-SAN.</u>** Prepare to counter punch lowering your body with the sinewave.

4. **<u>DO-SAN.</u>** Still in a left walking stance deliver a middle section reverse punch. **Gunnun sogi kaunde bandae jirugi.**

5. **<u>DO-SAN.</u>** Prepare to do a sharp turn to the right to be ready to block an attack. Arms raised with palms facing outwards.

6. **<u>DO-SAN.</u>** Turn 180 degrees into right walking stance, outer forearm high section side block. **Gunnun sogi, bakat palmok nopunde yop makgi.**

7. <u>DO-SAN.</u> In the walking stance, middle section reverse punch.
Gunnun sogi, kaunde bandae jirugi.

8. <u>DO-SAN.</u> Turn 90 degrees to the left into right L-stance, knife hand middle section guarding block. **Niunja sogi, sonkal kaunde daebi makgi.**

9. **<u>DO-SAN.</u>** Get ready to attack by moving the right foot forward and both fists at shoulder height.

10. <u>DO-SAN.</u> Attack from a right walking stance, middle section straight fingertip thrust. **Gunnun sogi, kaunde sun sonkut tulgi.** Shout **KIHAP!**

11. <u>DO-SAN.</u> Grab and twist the attacking hand downwards to the left.

12. <u>DO-SAN.</u> Pivot on the right foot to turn left with crossed forearms with the left underneath the right and both palms facing outwards.

13. DO-SAN. Finish the 360 degrees turn to the left into left walking stance, back fist high section side strike. **Gunnun sogi, dung joomuk nopunde yop taerigi.**

14. **DO-SAN.** Step forward with the right foot into right walking stance, back fist high section side strike. **Gunnun sogi, dung joomuk nopunde yop taerigi.**

15. <u>DO-SAN.</u> Turn 270 degrees to the left into a left walking stance, outer forearm high section side block. **Gunnun sogi, bakat palmok nopunde yop makgi.**

16. <u>DO-SAN.</u> Attack from the left walking stance, middle section reverse punch. **Gunnun sogi, kaunde bandae jirugi.**

17. <u>DO-SAN.</u> Turn to the right 180 degrees to block from a right walking stance, outer forearm high section block. **Gunnun sogi, bakat palmok nopunde yop makgi.**

18. <u>DO-SAN.</u> Attack from a right walking stance, middle section reverse punch. **Gunnun sogi, kaunde bandae jirugi.**

19. <u>DO-SAN.</u> Turn 135 degrees to the left with crossed forearms, left arm outwards and palms facing inwards - ready ...

20. <u>DO-SAN.</u> ... to step into left walking stance, outer forearm high section wedging block. **Gunnun sogi, bakat palmok nopunde hechyo makgi.**

21. <u>DO-SAN.</u> Keeping your arms held high, attack with right middle section front snap kick. **Kaunde apcha busigi.**

22. <u>DO-SAN.</u> Pull back the kicking leg with the right fist by the hip ready to ...

23. <u>DO-SAN.</u> ... attack with a right walking stance and with a raised left heel deliver a middle section punch. **Gunnun sogi, kaunde ap jirugi.**

24. <u>DO-SAN.</u> Immediately drop the left heel and still in right walking stance, attack with a middle section reverse punch. **Gunnun sogi, kaunde bandae jirugi.**

25. <u>DO-SAN.</u> Turn 90 degrees to the right into right walking stance, outer forearm high section wedging block. **Gunnun sogi, bakat palmok nopunde hechyo makgi.**

26. <u>DO-SAN.</u> With arms held high, palms forward, attack with a left middle section front snap kick. **Kaunde apcha busigi.**

27. <u>DO-SAN.</u> Step forward into left walking stance, with raised right heel, and prepare a middle section punch. **Gunnun sogi, kaunde ap jirugi.**

28. <u>DO-SAN.</u> As the heel comes down, still in left walking stance, attack with a middle section reverse punch. **Gunnun sogi, kaunde bandae jirugi.**

29. <u>DO-SAN.</u> Turn 45 degrees to the left and step into left walking stance and left forearm rising block. **Gunnun sogi, bakat palmok chookyo makgi.**

30. <u>DO-SAN.</u> Step forward into right walking stance with right forearm rising block. **Gunnun sogi, bakat palmok chookyo makgi.** Shout **KIHAP!**

31. <u>DO-SAN.</u> Pivot 270 degrees to the left, knees slightly bent, hands back-to-back with the right forward to prepare for knife hand side strike.

32. <u>DO-SAN.</u> Turning left, the left foot follows an arc over the floor and...

33. DO-SAN. ... finish with left sitting stance, knife hand side strike. **Gunnun sogi, sunkal yop taerigi.**

34. DO-SAN. Move left foot back in an arc back to the right, knees slightly bent, raised hands with the right forward with palms facing outward and looking right to ...

35. <u>DO-SAN.</u> ... a right sitting stance, knife hand side strike. **Annun sogi, sonkal yop taerigi. SHOUT KIHAP! ...** and then shout **Do-Sa**n.

36. <u>DO-SAN.</u> Bring the right foot back into parallel ready stance to finish. **Narani junbi sogi.**

WON-HYO

(Green belt, blue stripe)

Won-Hyo was the noted monk who introduced Buddhism to the Silla Dynasty in the year 686 AD.

1. **WON-HYO.** Begin with the close ready stance A. **Moa gunnun sogi A.**

2. **WON-HYO.** Turn 90 degrees to the left into right L-stance, twin forearm block. **Niunja sogi, sang palmok makgi.**

3. <u>**WON-HYO.**</u> Prepare for ....

4. <u>**WON-HYO**</u> ... coming out of the sine wave into right L-stance, right knife hand high section inwards strike. **Niunja sogi, sonkal nopunde taerigi.**

5. <u>**WON-HYO.**</u> Bring left back, right fist forward, left fist to the hip preparing to ...

6. <u>**WON-HYO.**</u> ... move the left foot forward into fixed-stance, middle section side punch. **Gojung sogi, kaunde yop jirugi.**

7. **WON-HYO.** Turn 180 degrees to the right, bring the right foot back with hands (palms facing inwards) ready for twin forearm block. **Sang palmok makgi.**

8. **WON-HYO.** Move the right foot into left L-stance, a twin forearm block. **Niunja sogi, sang palmok makgi.**

9. **WON-HYO.** Left L-stance, knife hand high section inward strike.
Niunja sogi, sonkal nopunde anuro taerigi.

10. **WON-HYO.** Right foot forward into right fixed stance, middle section
side punch. **Gojung sogi, kaunde yop jirugi.**

11. <u>WON-HYO.</u> Turn 90 degrees to the right into right bending ready stance. **Guburyo junbi sogi.**

12. <u>WON-HYO.</u> Sorry I can't kick this high, so I thought I'd have some fun and draw it (and others). Left middle section side piercing kick. **Kaunde yopcha jirugi.**

13. <u>WON-HYO.</u> Right L-stance, knife hand middle section guarding block. **Niunja sogi, sonkal kaunde daebi makgi.**

14. <u>WON-HYO.</u> Right foot forward into left L-stance, knife hand middle section
guarding block. **Niunja sogi, sonkal kaunde daebi makgi.**

15. <u>WON-HYO.</u> Left foot forward into right L-stance, knife hand middle section guarding block. **Niunja sogi, sonkal kaunde daebi makgi.**

16. <u>WON-HYO.</u> Right foot forward into right walking stance, middle section straight fingertip thrust. **Gunnun sogi, kaunde sun sonkut tulgi.** Then shout **KIHAP!**

17. <u>WON-HYO.</u> Turn 270 degrees to the left into right L-stance, twin forearm block.

Niunja sogi, sang palmok makgi.

18. <u>WON-HYO.</u> Sine wave into right L-stance, knife hand high section inward block.

Niunja sogi, sonkal nopunde anuro taerigi.

19. <u>WON-HYO.</u> Left foot forward into left fixed stance, middle section side punch.
Gojung sogi, kaunde yop jirugi.

20. <u>WON-HYO.</u> Turn 180 degrees to the right into left L-stance, twin forearm
block. **Niunja sogi, sang palmok makgi.**

21. <u>WON-HYO.</u> Raise your body and then drop into left L-stance knife, hand high section inward strike. **Niunja sogi, sonkal nopunde anuro taerigi.**

22. <u>WON-HYO.</u> Right fixed stance, middle section side punch. **Gojung sogi, kaunde yop jiruji.**

23. <u>WON-HYO.</u> Turn 90 degrees into left walking stance, inner forearm middle section circular block. **Gunnun sogi, an palmed kaunde dollimyo makgi.**

24. <u>WON-HYO.</u> Right low section front snap kick. **Najunde apcha busigi.**

25. <u>WON-HYO.</u> Right walking stance, middle section reverse punch.
Gunnun sogi, kaunde bandae jirigi.

26. <u>WON-HYO.</u> Right walking stance, inner forearm middle section circular block. **Gunnun sogi, an palmok kaunde dollimyo makgi.**

27. <u>WON-HYO.</u> Left low section front snap kick with hands in same position. **Najunde apcha busigi.**

28. <u>WON-HYO.</u> Left walking stance, middle section reverse punch. **Gunnun sogi, kaunde bandae jirugi.**

29. <u>WON-HYO.</u> Rise the right leg into left bending ready stance.
Guburyo junbi sogi.

30. <u>WON-HYO.</u> The drawing again! (All high kicks will be drawings).
Right middle section side piercing kick. **Kaunde yopcha jirugi.**

31. <u>WON-HYO.</u> Turn 170 degrees to the left into right L-stance, forearm middle
section guarding block. **Niunja sogi, palmok kaunde daebi makgi.**

32. <u>WON-HYO.</u> Turn 180 degrees to the right into left L-stance, forearm
middle section guarding block. **Niunja sogi, palmok kaunde daebi
makgi.** Then shout **KIHAP** and **Won-Hyo!**

33. <u>WON-HYO.</u> Finish with the right leg back into close ready stance. **Moa junbi sogi A.**

YUL-GOK

(Blue belt)

Yul-Gok is the pseudonym of the great philosopher and scholar Yi I (1536 – 1584), nicknamed the 'Confucius of Korea.' The thirty-eight movements of this pattern refer to his birthplace on the 38th degree latitude and the diagram of the pattern represents 'scholar.'

1. **Yul-Gok.** Parallel ready stance. **Narani junbi sogi.**

2. **Yul-Gok.** Swing the left foot in an arc into sitting stance **(Annun sogi)** with the left arm and clenched fist straight forward.

3. **Yul-Gok.** Rise and drop your body into sitting stance, middle section right punch. **Annun sogi, kaunde ap jirugi.** - then quickly into the following punch ...

4. **Yul-Gok.** Rise and drop again into sitting stance, middle section left punch. **Annun sogi, kaunde ap jirugi.** This and the previous punch are delivered as one fast movement.

5. __Yul-Gok.__ Swing left foot in an arc to the right, knees bent with right wrist on top of the left.

6. __Yul-Gok.__ Swing the right foot in an arc into sitting stance **(Annun sogi)** with the right arm and clenched fist straight forward.

7. **Yul-Gok.** Rise and drop into sitting stance with the left arm and clenched fist straight forward. **Annun sogi, kaunde ap jirugi.** - then quickly into the following punch ...

8. **Yul-Gok.** Rise and drop into sitting stance with the right arm and clenched right straight forward. **Annun sogi, kaunde ap jirugi.** This and the previous punch are delivered as one fast movement.

9. **<u>Yul-Gok.</u>** Step forward 45 degrees into walking stance, inner forearm middle section block. **Gunnun sogi, an palmok kaunde makgi.**

10. **<u>Yul-Gok.</u>** Left low section front snap kick. **Najunde apcha busigi.**

11. <u>Yul-Gok.</u> Raise right heel - left walking stance, middle section punch. **Gunnun sogi, kaunde ap jirugi.**

12. <u>Yul-Gok.</u> Push the heel down - left walking stance, middle section reverse punch. **Gunnun sogi, kaunde bandae jirugi.** This movement is delivered quickly as a continuum with the previous stance.

13. <u>Yul-Gok.</u> Turn the right foot 90 degrees to the right and step forward into left walking stance, inner forearm middle section block. **Gunnun sogi, an palmok kaunde makgi.**

14. <u>Yul-Gok.</u> Right low section front snap kick. **Najunde apcha busigi.**

15. <u>Yul-Gok.</u> Raise left heel, right walking stance, middle section punch.
Gunnun sogi, kaunde ap jirugi.

16. <u>Yul-Gok.</u> Push the heel down - right walking stance, middle section reverse punch. **Gunnun sogi, kaunde bandae jirugi.** This movement is delivered quickly as a continuum with the previous stance.

17. <u>Yul-Gok.</u> Turn 45 degrees to the right with hands back-to-back and the right hand open.

18. <u>Yul-Gok.</u> Step into right walking stance, palm middle section hooking block. **Gunnun sogi, sonbadak kaunde golcho makgi.**

19. <u>Yul-Gok.</u> Raise left heel - right walking stance, middle hooking block. Palm downwards. **Gunnun sogi, sonbadak kaunde golcho makgi.**

20. <u>Yul-Gok.</u> Push the heel down - right walking stance, middle section punch. **Gunnun sogi, kaunde ap jirugi.** This movement is delivered quickly as a continuum with the previous stance.

21. <u>Yul-Gok.</u> Step forward into left walking stance, palm middle section hooking block. Palm downwards. **Gunnun sogi, sonbadak kaunde golcho makgi.**

22. <u>Yul-Gok.</u> Raise the body from the right foot into left walking stance, palm middle section hooking block with the right palm downwards. **Gunnun sogi, sonbadak kaunde golcho makgi.**

23. Yul-Gok. Right heal down into left walking stance, middle section punch. **Gunnun sogi, kaunde ap jirugi.** This movement is delivered quickly as a continuum with the previous stance.

24. Yul-Gok. Step into right walking stance, middle section punch. **Gunnun sogi, kaunde ap jirugi.**

25. <u>Yul-Gok.</u> Left foot raised into right ready bending stance.
Guburyo sogi.

26. <u>Yul-Gok.</u> Left middle section side piercing kick.
Kaunde yopcha jirugi.

27. <u>Yul-Gok.</u> Step forward into left walking stance, front elbow strike. **Gunnun sogi, ap palkup taerigi.** Shout **KIHAP!** The right elbow strikes the left palm.

28. <u>Yul-Gok.</u> Turn 180 degrees to the right with left foot raised into left bending ready stance. **Guburyo sogi.**

29. <u>Yul-Gok.</u> Right middle section side piercing kick. **Kaunde yopcha jirugi.**

30. <u>Yul-Gok.</u> Step forward into right walking stance, front elbow strike. **Gunnun sogi, ap palkup taerigi.** Shout **KIHAP!** The left elbow strikes the right palm.

31. <u>Yul-Gok.</u> Turn 90 degrees to the left into right L-stance, twin knife hand block. **Niunja sogi, sang sonkal makgi.**

32. <u>Yul-Gok.</u> Right walking stance, straight fingertip thrust. **Gunnun sogi, sun sonkut tulgi.**

33. <u>Yul-Gok.</u> Turn 180 degrees to the right into right L-stance, twin knife hand block. **Niunja sogi, sang sonkal makgi.**

34. <u>Yul-Gok.</u> Step into left walking stance, fingertip thrust. **Gunnun sogi, sun sonkut tulgi.**

35. <u>Yul-Gok.</u> Turn 90 degrees into left walking stance, outer forearm high section side block. **Gunnun sogi, bakat palmok nopunde yop makgi.**

36. <u>Yul-Gok.</u> Raise your body by the right foot and force your heel down into left walking stance, middle section reverse punch. **Gunnun sogi, kaunde bandae jirugi.**

37. <u>Yul-Gok.</u> Step into right walking stance, outer forearm high section side block. **Gunnun sogi, bakat palmok nopunde yop makgi.**

38. <u>Yul-Gok.</u> Raise your body by the left foot and force your heel down into right walking stance, middle section reverse punch. **Gunnun sogi, kaunde bandae jirugi.**

39. <u>Yul-Gok.</u> Jump back into left X-stance, back fist high section side strike. Right raised heel. **Kyocha sogi, dung joomuk nopunde yop taerigi.**

40. <u>Yul-Gok.</u> Turn 270 degrees into right walking stance, double forearm high section block. **Gunnun sogi, doo palmok nopunde makgi.**

41. <u>Yul-Gok.</u> Turn 180 degrees into left walking stance, double forearm high section block. **Gunnun sogi, doo palmok nopunde makgi.** Shout – **KIHAP!** and **YUL-GOK!**

42. <u>Yul-Gok.</u> Left leg back into ready parallel ready stance. **Narani junbi sogi.**

JOONG-GUN

(Blue belt, RED STRIPE)

Joon-Gun is named after the patriot Ahn Joong-Gun who assassinated Hiro-Bumi Ito, the first Japanese governor-general of Korea, who played a leading part in the Korea-Japan merger. There are thirty-two movements in this pattern to represent Ahn Joong-Gun's age when he was executed at Lui-Shung prison in 1910.

1. **JOONG-GUN.** Closed ready stance B. **Moa junbi sogi B.**

2. **JOONG-GUN.** Turn 90 degrees with left foot into right L-stance, reverse knife hand middle section side block. **Niunja sogi, sonkal dung kaunde yop makgi.**

3. **JOONG-GUN.** Left low section side front snap kick. **Najunde yopapcha busigi.**

4. **JOONG-GUN.** Step forward into left rear foot stance, palm upward block. **Dwitbal sogi, sonbadak ollyo makgi.**

5. <u>**JOONG-GUN.**</u> Turn 180 degrees stepping into left L-stance, reverse knife hand middle section side block. **Niunja sogi, sonkal dung kaunde yop makgi.**

6. <u>**JOONG-GUN.**</u> Right low section side front snap kick. **Najunde yopapcha busigi.**

7. **JOONG-GUN.** Right rear foot stance, palm upward block. **Dwitbal sogi, sonbadak ollyo makgi.**

8. **JOONG-GUN.** Turn 90 degrees into right L-stance, knife hand middle section guarding block. **Niunja sogi, sonkal kaunde daebi makgi.**

9. **JOONG-GUN.** Left walking stance, upper elbow strike. **Gunnun sogi, wi palkup taerigi.**

10. **JOONG-GUN.** Right foot forward into left L-stance, knife hand middle section guarding block. **Niunja sogi, sonkal kaunde daebi makgi.**

11. <u>JOONG-GUN.</u> Right walking stance, upper elbow strike. **Gunnun sogi, wi palkup taerigi.**

12. <u>JOONG-GUN.</u> Left step forward into left walking stance, high section twin vertical punch. **Gunnun sogi, nopunde sang sewo jirugi.**

13. <u>JOONG-GUN.</u> Right step forward into right walking stance, twin upset punch. **Gunnun sogi, sang dwijibo jirugi. ...** Shout **KIHAP!**

14. <u>JOONG-GUN.</u> Turn 180 degrees, fists ready at waist height to ...

15. <u>JOONG-GUN.</u> ... cross over as they rise into left walking stance, X-fist rising block. **Gunnun sogi, kyocha joomuk chookyo makgi.**

16. <u>JOONG-GUN.</u> Turn 90 degrees into right L-stance, back fist high section left hand side strike. **Niunja sogi, dung joomuk nopunde yop taerigi.**

17. <u>JOONG-GUN.</u> Turn left fist downwards, left walking stance. **Niunja sogi.**

18. <u>JOONG-GUN.</u> Rise up and down on right foot into left walking stance, high section reverse punch. **Gunnun sogi, nopunde bandae jirugi.**

19. <u>JOONG-GUN.</u> Turn 180 degrees into left L-stance, back fist high section side strike. **Niunja sogi, dung joomuk nopunde yop taerigi.**

20. <u>JOONG-GUN.</u> Right walking stance with downwards back fist.
Niunja sogi.

21. <u>JOONG-GUN.</u> Right walking stance, high section reverse punch. Executed as one quick motion with the previous stance rising up and down on left foot. **Gunnun sogi, nopunde bandae jirugi.**

22. <u>JOONG-GUN.</u> Turn 90 degrees into left walking stance, double forearm high section block. **Gunnun sogi, doo palmok nopunde makgi.**

23. <u>JOONG-GUN.</u> Right L-stance, middle section side punch. **Niunja sogi, kaunde yop jirugi.**

24. <u>JOONG-GUN.</u> Middle section side piercing kick.
Kaunde yopcha jirugi.

25. <u>JOONG-GUN.</u> Right walking stance, double forearm high section block. **Gunnun sogi, doo palmok nopunde makgi.**

26. <u>JOONG-GUN.</u> Right foot back into left L-stance, middle section side punch. **Niunja sogi, kaunde yop jirugi.**

27. <u>JOONG-GUN.</u> Pivot on the right foot for a left middle section side piercing kick. **Kaunde yopcha jirugi.**

28. <u>JOONG-GUN.</u> Right L-stance, forearm middle section guarding block. **Niunja sogi, palmok kaunde darbi makgi.**

29. <u>JOONG-GUN.</u> Left foot back, arms at wait height with palms facing each other ready to ...

30. <u>JOONG-GUN.</u> ... slowly perform left low stance, palm pressing block. **Nachuo sogi, sonbadak noollo makgi.**

31. <u>JOONG-GUN.</u> Step forward into left L-stance, forearm middle section guarding block. **Niunja sogi, palmok kaunde daebi makgi.**

32. <u>JOONG-GUN.</u> Right low stance, palm pressing block. **Nachuo sogi, sonbadak noollo makgi.**

33. <u>JOONG-GUN.</u> Turn 90 degrees to the right for close stance, angle punch. **Moa sogi, giokja jirugi.**

34. <u>JOONG-GUN.</u> Right fixed stance, U-shape block. **Gojung sogi, digutja makgi.**

35. <u>JOONG-GUN.</u> Left fixed stance, U-shape block. **Gojung sogi, digutja makgi.** Shout **KIHAP! ...** then **JOONG-GUN!**

36. <u>JOONG-GUN.</u> Close ready stance B. **Moa junbi sogi B.**

TOI-GYE

(Red belt)

Toi-Gye is the pen name of the noted scholar Yi Hwang (Sixteenth Century), an authority on Neo-Confucianism. The thirty-seven movements of this pattern refer to his birthplace on the 37th degree latitude and the diagram represents 'scholar.'

1. **TOI-GYE.** Close ready stance B. **Moa junbi sogi B.**

2. **TOI-GYE**. Turn 90 degrees into right L-stance, inner forearm middle section block. **Niunja sogi an plamok kaunde makgi.**

3. **TOI-GYE.** With your palm upwards step into left walking stance, upset fingertip thrust. **Gunnun sogi, dwijibun sonkut tulgi.**

4. **TOI-GYE**. Turn 90 degrees to the right with arms crossed at chest height, the right one underneath, ready to ...

5. <u>**TOI-GYE.**</u> ... to use the right fist striking a back fist side back strike, in the close stance. **Moa sogi, dung joomuk yopdwi taerigi.**

6. <u>**TOI-GYE**</u>. Turn 90 degrees to the right into left L-stance, inner forearm middle section block. **Niunja sogi, an palmok kaunde makgi.**

7. **TOI-GYE.** With right foot, step into right walking stance, upset fingertip thrust. **Gunnun sogi, dwijibun sonkut tulgi.**

8. **TOI-GYE**. Bring the right foot into close stance, back fist side back strike. **Moa sogi, dung joomuk yopdwi taerigi.**

9. **TOI-GYE.** Left walking stance, X-fist pressing block. **Gunnun sogi, kyocha joomuk noollo makgi.**

10. TOI-GYE. Fists chest height with inward facing palms ready ...

11. <u>TOI-GYE</u> ... to attack from left walking stance with high section twin vertical punch. **Gunnun sogi, nopunde sang sewo jirugi.**

12. <u>TOI-GYE.</u> Right middle section front snap kick. **Kaunde apcha busigi.**

13. <u>TOI-GYE.</u> Right walking stance, middle section punch. **Gunnun sogi, kaunde ap jirugi.**

14. <u>TOI-GYE.</u> Still in right walking stance deliver a left middle section reverse punch. **Gunnun sogi, kaunde bandae jurugi.**

15. <u>TOI-GYE.</u> Turn 90 degrees to the left into close stance, twin side elbow thrust. **Moa sogi, sang yop palkup tulgi.**

16. <u>TOI-GYE.</u> Turn 90 degrees to the left stamping the right foot down into sitting stance, W-shape block. **Annun sogi, san makgi.**

17. <u>TOI-GYE.</u> Turn 180 degrees to the right stamping the left foot into sitting stance, W-shape block. **Annun sogi, san makgi.**

18. <u>TOI-GYE.</u> Turn 180 degrees to the right stamping the left foot into sitting stance, W-shape block. **Annun sogi, san makgi.**

19. <u>TOI-GYE.</u> Turn 180 degrees to the left stamping the right foot down into sitting stance, W-shape block. **Annun sogi, san makgi.**

20. <u>TOI-GYE.</u> Turn 180 degrees to the right stamping the left foot into sitting stance, W-shape block. **Annun sogi, san makgi.**

21. TOI-GYE. Turn 180 degrees to the right stamping the left foot into sitting stance, W-shape block. **Annun sogi, san makgi.**

22. TOI-GYE. Turn 90 degrees to the right with fists shoulder height and palms facing outward to ...

23. <u>TOI-GYE.</u> ... step into a right L-stance, double forearm low section pushing block. **Niunja sogi, doo palmok najunde miro makgi.**

24. <u>TOI-GYE</u>. Left walking stance **(Gunnun sogi)** with open hands to grab an attacker's head.

25. <u>TOI-GYE</u>. .. as if holding an attacker's head pull hands downwards into a knee upward kick. **Moorup ollyo chagi.**

26. <u>TOI-GYE</u>. Turn 180 degrees to the left into right L-stance, knife hand middle section guarding block. **Niunja sogi, sonkal kaunde daebi makgi.**

27. <u>TOI-GYE.</u> Low section side front snap kick. **Najunde yop apcha busigi .**

28. <u>TOI-GYE.</u> Left walking stance, flat fingertip high section thrust. **Gunnun sogi, opun sonkut nopunde tulgi.**

29. <u>TOI-GYE.</u> Left L-stance, knife hand middle section guarding block.
Niunja sogi, sonkal kaunde daebi makgi.

30. <u>TOI-GYE.</u> Low section side front snap kick. **Najunde yop apcha busigi.**

31. <u>TOI-GYE.</u> Right walking stance, flat fingertip high section thrust.
Gunnun sogi, opun sonkut nopunde tulgi.

32. <u>TOI-GYE.</u> Step back into right L-stance, back fist side back strike.
Niunja sogi, dung joomuk yopdwi taerigi and **bakat palmok najunde makgi.**

33. <u>TOI-GYE.</u> Jump forward into right X-stance, pushing down with right X-fist pressing block. **Kyocha sogi, koycha joomuk noollo makgi. ...** shout **KIHAP!**

34. <u>TOI-GYE.</u> Right walking stance, double forearm high section block. **Gunnun sogi, doo palmok nopunde makgi.**

35. <u>TOI-GYE.</u> Turn 270 degrees to the left into right L-stance, knife hand low section guarding block. **Niunja sogi, sonkal najunde daebi makgi.**

36. <u>TOI-GYE</u>. Left walking stance, inner forearm middle section circular block. **Gunnun sogi, an palmok kaunde dollimyo makgi.**

37. <u>TOI-GYE</u>. Turn 180 degrees to the right into left L-stance, knife hand low section guarding block. **Niunja sogi, sonkal najunde daebi makgi.**

38. <u>TOI-GYE.</u> Right walking stance, inner forearm middle section circular block. **Gunnun sogi, an palmok kaunde dollimyo makgi.**

39. <u>TOI-GYE.</u> Left walking stance, inner forearm middle section circular block. **Gunnun sogi, an palmok kaunde dollimyo makgi.**

40. <u>TOI-GYE.</u> Right walking stance, inner forearm middle section circular block. **Gunnun sogi, an palmok kaunde dollimyo makgi.**

41. <u>TOI-GYE.</u> Turn 90 degrees into sitting stance, middle section punch. **Annun sogi, kaunde ap jirugi.** Shout **KIHAP!** and then shout **TOI-GYE.**

42. <u>TOI-GYE.</u> Close ready stance B. **Moa junbi sogi B**.

HWA-RANG

(Red belt/black stripe)

Hwa-Rang is named after the Hwa-Rang youth group that originated in the Silla Dynasty in the early seventh century. The twenty-nine movements of the pattern refer to the 29th Infantry Division where Taekwondo developed into maturity.

1. HWA-RANG. Close ready stance B. **Moa junbi sogi B.**

2. HWA-RANG. Move left leg sideways into sitting stance, middle section pushing block. **Annun sogi, sonbadak kaunde miro makgi.**

3.   HWA-RANG. Sitting stance, right arm middle section front punch.
Annun sogi, kaunde ap jirugi.

4.   HWA-RANG. Sitting stance, left arm middle section front punch.
Annun sogi, kaunde ap jirugi.

5. **HWA-RANG.** Rising slightly turn 90 degrees to the right into left L-stance, twin forearm block. **Niunja sogi, sang palmok makgi.**

6. **HWA-RANG.** Rise slightly with fists ...

7. **HWA-RANG.** ... when in left L-stance, bought inward with the right-side fist on the left shoulder. **Niunja sogi, so ollyo jirugi.**

8. **HWA-RANG.** Left foot into right fixed stance, middle section punch. **Gojung sogi, kaunde yop jirugi.**

9. <u>HWA-RANG.</u> Right foot back moving right knife hand overhead
ready ...

10. <u>HWA-RANG.</u> ... attack, when in a left vertical stance, with knife hand
downward strike. **Soojik sogi, sonkal naeryo taerigi.**

11. <u>HWA-RANG.</u> Left leg into left walking stance, middle section punch.
Gunnun sogi, kaunde ap jirugi.

12. <u>HWA-RANG.</u> Turn 90 degrees to the left into walking stance, outer forearm low section block. **Gunnun sogi, bakat palmok najunde makgi.**

13. <u>HWA-RANG.</u> Step into right leg walking stance, middle section punch. **Gunnun sogi, kaunde ap jirugi.**

14. <u>HWA-RANG.</u> Lower your body, cover your right fist with left palm.

15. <u>HWA-RANG.</u> Middle section side piercing kick pulling upper torso backwards. **Kaunde yop cha jirugi.**

16. <u>HWA-RANG.</u> Right leg down into left L-stance, knife hand side strike. **Niunja sogi, sonkal yop taerigi.**

17. <u>HWA-RANG.</u> Step into left walking stance, middle section punch.
Gunnun sogi, kaunde ap jirugi.

18. <u>HWA-RANG.</u> Step into right walking stance, middle section punch.
Gunnun sogi, kaunde ap jirugi. ... and shout **KIHAP!**

19. <u>HWA-RANG.</u> Turn 270 degrees into right L-stance, knife hand middle section guarding block. **Niunja sogi, sonkal kaunde daebi makgi.**

20. <u>HWA-RANG.</u> Step into right walking stance, straight fingertip thrust. **Gunnun sogi, sun sonkut tulgi.**

21. HWA-RANG. Turn 180 degrees to the left into right L-stance, knife hand middle section guarding block. **Niunja sogi, sonkal kaunde daebi makgi.**

22. HWA-RANG. Right high turning kick. **Nopunde dollyo chagi.**

23. <u>HWA-RANG.</u> Left high turning kick. **Nopunde dollyo chagi.**

24. <u>HWA-RANG.</u> Right L-stance, knife hand middle section guarding block. **Niunja sogi, sonkal kaunde daebi makgi.**

25. <u>HWA-RANG.</u> Turn 90 degrees into left walking stance, outer forearm low section block. **Gunnun sogi, bakat palmok najunde makgi.**

26. <u>HWA-RANG.</u> Right L-stance, middle section punch. **Niunja sogi, kaunde ap jirugi.**

27. <u>HWA-RANG.</u> Left L-stance, middle section punch. **Niunja sogi, kaunde ap jirugi.**

28. <u>HWA-RANG.</u> Right L-stance, middle section punch. **Niunja sogi, kaunde ap jirugi.**

29. <u>HWA-RANG.</u> Left walking stance, X-fist pressing block with right fist on top. **Gunnun sogi, kyocha joomuk noollo makgi.**

30. <u>HWA-RANG.</u> Turn 180 to the left and cross the right arm underneath the left ready to ...

31. <u>HWA-RANG.</u> ... slide the right foot forward into right L-stance, side elbow thrust. **Niunja sogi, yop palkup tulgi. ...** and then shout **KIHAP!**

32. <u>HWA-RANG.</u> Turn 90 degrees to the left into close stance, inner forearm side front block with the right arm **(Moa sogi, an palmok yopap makgi)** and with an outer forearm low section block with the left arm. **Bakat palmok najunde makgi.**

33. <u>HWA-RANG.</u> Rise body and fall into close stance, inner forearm side front block with the left arm **(Moa sogi, an palmok yopap makgi)** and with an outer forearm low section block with the right arm. **Bakat palmok najunde makgi.**

34. <u>HWA-RANG.</u> Left foot forward into right L-stance, knife hand middle section block. **Niunja sogi, sonkal kaunde daebi makgi.**

35. <u>HWA-RANG.</u> Turn 180 degrees to the right into right L-stance, knife hand middle section guarding block and **...** shout **KIHAP!** and then **HWA-RANG!**

36. <u>HWA-RANG.</u> Right leg back into close ready stance. **Moa junbi sogi B.**

CHOONG-MOO
(Black belt)

Choong-Moo was the name given to the great admiral Yi Soon-sin of the Yi dynasty who was reputed to have invented the first armoured battleship (Kobukson) in 1952 which is said to be the precursor of the present-day submarine. The reason why this pattern ends with a left-handed attack is to symbolize his regrettable death: he was never allowed to reach his full potential as he was forced to be loyal to the king.

1. **CHOOG-MOO.** Parallel ready stance. **Narani junbi sogi.**

2. **CHOONG-MOO.** Turn 90 degrees left into right L-stance, twin hand knife block. **Niunja sogi, sang sonkal makgi.**

3. CHOONG-MOO. Stepping forward with the right leg, head-high fists facing outwards ready ..

4. CHOONG-MOO. .. for right walking stance, knife hand high section inward strike. **Gunnun sogi, nopunde anuro taerigi.**

5. <u>CHOONG-MOO.</u> Turn 180 degrees to the right into left L-stance, knife hand middle section guarding block. **Niunja sogi, kaunde daebi makgi.**

6. <u>CHOONG-MOO.</u> Left walking stance, flat fingertip high section thrust. **Gunnun sogi, so opun sonkut nopunde tulgi.**

7. <u>CHOONG-MOO</u>. Turn 90 degrees to the left into L-stance, middle section guarding block. **Niunja sogi, sonkal kaunde daebi makgi.**

8. <u>CHOONG-MOO.</u> Turn 180 degrees to the right bringing up the right leg into left bending ready stance. **Guburyo sogi.**

9. <u>CHOONG-MOO.</u> Middle section side piercing kick.
Kaunde yopcha jirugi.

10. <u>CHOONG-MOO.</u> Turn 180 degrees to the left into right L-stance, knife hand middle section guarding block. **Niunja sogi, sonkal kaunde daebi makgi.**

11. <u>CHOONG-MOO.</u> Step forward with right leg and then ...

12. <u>CHOONG-MOO.</u> ... leap into the air with the legs tucked in ready to...

13. <u>CHOONG-MOO.</u> ... attack with a flying side piercing kick.
Twimyo yopcha jirugi.

14. <u>CHOONG-MOO.</u> Left L-stance, knife hand middle section guarding block. **Niunja sogi, so sonkal daebi makgi.** Then shout **KIHAP!**

15. <u>CHOONG-MOO</u>. Turn 270 degrees to the left into right L-stance, outer forearm low section block. **Niunja sogi, bakat palmok najunde makgi.**

16. <u>CHOONG-MOO</u>. Left walking stance, both arms extending to grab an attacker's neck ...

17. <u>CHOONG-MOO</u>. ... and pull downwards as executing a knee upward kick. **Moorup ollyo chagi.**

18. <u>CHOONG-MOO.</u> Turn 180 degrees into left walking stance, reverse knife hand high section front strike. **Gunnun sogi, sonkal dung nopunde ap taerigi.**

19. <u>CHOONG-MOO.</u> High section turning kick. **Nopunde dollyo chagi.**

20. <u>CHOONG-MOO.</u> Turn 180 degrees to the right for a middle section back piercing kick. **Kaunde dwitcha jirugi.**

21. <u>CHOONG-MOO.</u> Left L-stance, forearm middle section guarding block. **Niunja sogi, palmok kaunde daebi makgi.**

22. <u>CHOONG-MOO.</u> Left leg middle section turning kick. **Kaunde dollyo chagi.**

23. <u>CHOONG-MOO.</u> Turn 90 degrees to the right into fixed stance u-shaped block. **Gojung so diguta makgi.**

24. <u>CHOONG-MOO.</u> Leap straight upwards with both legs tucked in as ...

25. <u>CHOONG-MOO.</u> ... you turn a complete 360 degree circle to land in...

26. <u>CHOONG-MOO.</u> ... a left L-stance, , knife hand middle section guarding block. **Niunja sogi, sonkal kaunde daebi makgi.**

27. <u>CHOONG-MOO.</u> Step into left walking stance, upset fingertip thrust.
Gunnun sogi, dwijibun sonkut tulgi.

28. <u>CHOONG-MOO.</u> Right L-stance, back fist side back strike. **Niunja sogi, dung joomuk nopunde yop taerigi.**

29. <u>CHOONG-MOO.</u> Right walking stance, straight fingertip thrust. **Gunnun sogi, sun sonkut tulgi.**

30. <u>**CHOONG-MOO.**</u> Turn 270 degrees to the left into left walking stance, double forearm high section block. **Gunnun sogi, doo palmok nopunde makgi.**

31. <u>CHOONG-MOO.</u> Turn 90 degrees to the left into sitting stance, inner forearm middle section front block. **Annun sogi, an palmok kaunde ap makgi.**

32. <u>CHOONG-MOO.</u> Sitting stance, back fist high section side strike. **Annun sogi, dung joomuk nopunde yop taerigi.**

33. <u>CHOONG-MOO.</u> Turn 90 degrees to the left and deliver a right middle section side piercing kick. **Kaunde yopcha jirugi.**

34. <u>CHOONG-MOO.</u> ... and then a left middle section side piercing kick. **Kaunde yopcha jirugi.**

35. <u>CHOONG-MOO.</u> Turn 180 degrees to the right into a left L-stance, x-knife hand checking block. **Niunja sogi, kyocha sonkal momchau makgi.**

36. <u>CHOONG-MOO.</u> Step into a left walking stance, palm upward block. **Gunnun sogi, sang sonbadak ollyo makgi.**

37. <u>CHOONG-MOO.</u> Turn 180 degrees to the right into walking stance, outer forearm rising block. **Gunnun sogi, bakat palmok chookyo makgi.**

38. <u>CHOONG-MOO.</u> Walking stance, middle section reverse punch. **Gunnun sogi, kaunde bandae jirugi.** Shout **KIHAP! ...** and then **Choong-Moo.**

39. <u>CHOONG-MOO.</u> Finish back in parallel ready stance. **Narani junbi sogi.**

Thank you. **Gamsahabnida**

I hope you enjoyed the photos as much as I did - and the drawings. Sorry I couldn't do any of the high kicks for you – but the old body is not as agile as it once was. In the background is our beautiful Oxley Beach here in Port Macquarie. The rocky outcrop is known locally as Flagstaff. Come and visit.

W. HIDDEN MEANINGS OF TAEKWON-DO THINKING and POWER

1. The Importance of your Taekwon-do Journey

One of the eminent fathers of Chinese thinking the great philosopher Lao Tzu said, 'The journey of a thousand miles begins with one step.' This ancient wisdom is so true in its obvious simplicity and for all that it signifies. Firstly, it signifies the beginning – a journey that has started. No longer is the traveler stationary but has begun to move along a certain path, in a certain direction towards a certain goal.

Modern philosophers have pointed out the importance of enjoying the journey as much as reaching the goal. This is also wise. There is much to see and experience along the way. Indeed, for many travelers this is the reason they undertake their travels - to experience and to grow.

All journeys have goals, even those travelers who wander simply for its own sake mainly do so to attain a particular and often unorthodox perspective of life. This has been a tradition for various monks and mystics from many cultures for centuries. Whatever the purpose of the journey or whatever the final goal or destination may be, the nature of the journey is of equal importance.

That first step also determines the traveler's direction. Yes some might wander, but mainly people undertake a journey specifically to reach a set destination or to achieve a goal. That first step which becomes so much a part of the journey is what empowers the traveler on to success or on to arriving at journey's end.

When that first step is followed by another step, and another and another, it sets the foundation for the way ahead and must be repeated time and again in order for the journey to reach a happy and satisfying conclusion.

Lao Tzu's words contain much wisdom and are inexplicably entwined with Taekwon-do. The beginner starts with no knowledge of this dynamic Korean martial art. Just as a traveler starts with that one step - so does each and every Taekwon-do student start by learning the first basic movement of TKD.

That first basic movement is just as important to the student as to the first step of all travelers who have undertaken a thousand journeys. For Taekwon-do is also a journey. No less important, or thrilling than a geographical one, and most certainly every bit as exciting.

It is a journey that has different goals for different students. For many it is to gain the Black Belt, while for others it is to go on and complete all 24 patterns. Other students practice Taekwon-do to become masters while some do so to embrace the many benefits that Taekwon-do offers by enriching the mind and the body.

There are various reasons why so many people start their Taekwon-do life but it does not matter why. For whatever the reason or the particular goal, or destination the student has in mind they must take that first step. And keep taking it again and again for them to be enriched from their journey or to reach its ultimate end.

The first step in Taekwon-do is not only the act of beginning but learning the basics of the art so that they can be repeated almost countless times in order to experience, master and to achieve the desired final outcome.

ITF Taekwon-do's basics are embedded in the practice of all its patterns – as well as its theory. Both the practice and theory as bodies of discipline must be learnt until it is deeply engrained in muscle memory as well as the memory of the mind.

This handbook of ITF Taekwon-do's practice and theory is full of the basics. Essential basics to take that first step of the 'Thousand Mile' Taekwon-do journey and basics that form the foundation of each and every ITF Taekwon-do student's experience and learning - no matter how far they have progressed with their patterns or which colour belt they have attained.

Lao Tzu recognised the importance of the journey to an individual's life. So did General Choi Hong Hi the founder of ITF Taekwon-do. And, each of these great men knew the importance of the first step(s) - the basics. So too does the wise Taekwon-do student, which is why this handbook is a vital resource of information for each and every student.

2. The 4 point foundation of your Taekwon-do success

1. Setting a goal

It has been said that if you aim at nothing you will hit it every time. Nothing or nowhere is certainly not a good place to be or to be going to. Far better to have a goal and move towards hitting it, for goals set the direction before us and determine the outcome.

Of course there is much to enjoy and experience along the way that often deepens the journeyman's individual being as he, or she, moves onwards towards the target ahead. Which, would otherwise not have been experienced if that person had remained 'nowhere.'

However, moving towards an ultimate end is a powerful motivator as the vision ahead holds out an attainment that often glitters with much promise. For goals are where a prize awaits, be it one of great value or the fulfilment of an aimed-for-achievement, growth, maturity or possession of some kind.

For the Taekwon-do student, this is very important as the goal determines what the student wants out of the Taekwon-do life. Many students have different goals.

Some only want to achieve their black belt, while for others it's to embrace the much bigger picture across the broad spectrum of what Taekwon-do can offer, be that physical or mental health for example. Or, a deepening of one's self through immersion in the Taekwon-do life, culture and spirit.

2. Make a commitment

Once that goal is identified it's crucial that a commitment is made to reach it. For it will not come casually. As much as Taekwon-do is enjoyable with many fun moments along the way, it is not a game. Thus, with the intent of launching out to reach your ultimate prize, a serious commitment must be made. It cannot be otherwise.

There is so much to learn, so much to become - and so much that one inherits and ultimately must hold as a worthy steward as a Taekwon-do practitioner. For Taekwon-do is bigger than us all.

3. Lay a foundation.

Just as no building is raised up without a solid foundation, so too is nothing achieved in Taekwon-do without a firm base to build upon. For the 24 patterns found within ITF Taekwon-do are infused with the many stances, blocks, kicks, strikes and thrusts that are learnt with a continual repetition of the basics being performed many times.

Taekwon-do is like a mighty house with numerous rooms containing many treasures to be discovered. So, an enduring foundation must be laid. It will take time. For some, the seemingly endless training appears to be unnecessary and they may go elsewhere to seek other paths. However, this aspect is an essential and very vital part of training which must be laid down correctly.

It puts in place a foundation that in time supports and sustains the real depth, achievements and riches of what Taekwon-do offers.

And, perhaps this initial repetition is an example of General Choi Hong Hi testing the undisciplined or to impart some mettle into students so they can grow and progress with TKD. Quitting when something seems too hard does not empower nor assist in reaching your destination.

4. Become a life-long learner

Today in this modern age when change is all around us, it is not uncommon to hear the phrase, 'Being a life-long learner.' With the pace of this change moving so quickly and at times in unpredictable directions, jobs and the once held certainties of life are coming and going very quickly.

Today's jobs are gone tomorrow and tomorrow's jobs are yet to be created. To survive by making a living in this fast-paced age one has to be open, be able to adapt and ever-willing to learn. To be a life-long learner.

The true Taekwon-do student embraces this attribute. They are after all, just that - a student. However, unlike the ever-changing workplace, Taekwon-do has a firm curriculum that is lengthy, broad and firmly set.

It is at times slightly adjusted but General Choi Hong Hi has left a solid and lasting outline to this fascinating Korean Martial Art. Learning is part of becoming and part of reaching whatever goals students have set before themselves.

Becoming a life-long learner is also a gift that Taekwon-do bestows upon each student assisting them throughout their everyday life in order to help with their goals and achievements.

3. Crucial steps to Taekwon-do empowerment

Taekwon-do power is within each and every student. This is indeed good news as succeeding or having the power to do so in many sports is not always within reach of everyone. Not everyone has the correct athletic build or physical attributes to do well at a particular sport they may favour. However, everyone can succeed and reach their goals in Taekwon-do.

The art of Taekwon-do is not dependent upon body shape, strength or even ability. The power and ability to practice Taekwon-do is easily available for everyone, for it lies within each student - and is harnessed by a positive attitude of believing that, 'I can do it!'
Every student enjoying and achieving along the way of their TKD journey taps into this latent power that lies within themselves. It is as simple as a positive and focused mental application of not limiting oneself.

There are no barriers other than the lack of a willingness to ignite self-motivation and not accepting the self-belief that you can have success in achieving your TKD goals. For indeed all self-belief and positive attributes of self-improvement are readily available to us all.

Self-belief along with a commitment to being fit, studying the Taekwon-do curriculum and learning the patterns are essential to ensuring the best results from your Taekwon-do journey. Of course, there are many benefits students receive from training in their Dojong with their instructors and others. But, essentially Taekwon-do is for one's self, and as such must be powered by what the individual student draws from within one's own self.

Some of the best practitioners of Taekwon-do have odd body shapes that some would see as being far from an 'ideal athletic type.' These students and masters have simply learnt how to motivate themselves from within and so refuse to be limited, disadvantaged or to quit.

Nor should age be a barrier. Students in their 60's have won their black belts, gone onto various Dan levels and fought successfully in tournaments. Indeed, some of the best Taekwon-do exponents are of a ripe mature age. These students do not see obstacles in their way but rather choose to work with their bodies as they are. They train, study, learn, develop, practice and become powerful within the context of what their bodies can achieve. Self-belief and application are the sources of power which is found within each TKD student.

The question is often asked if Taekwon-do is a spiritual force. Does it have a spiritual dimension that students need to draw from to practice it? And the answer is - no, there isn't. There is no calling upon a larger power or entity somewhere out there to guide, to grant wisdom, or to give strength. As previously stated, much of the power needed to practice Taekwon-do comes from within the individual, just as it does for any athlete in whatever other sport they may be seeking to succeed in.

Tackwon-do as a Martial Art also draws its power from its challenging curriculum, intelligent body of theory, physical exercises and fascinating fighting patterns that make it such a dynamic practice. And as such, this body of knowledge is a powerful mix, that when added to the student's will becomes an unstoppable force.

Taekwon-do empowers lives to participate in the sport as well as a broader application to all other areas of living, just as a degree that is studied at university empowers a graduate's life.

Both TKD and university degrees are bigger than their students and as such, impart knowledge and ensure growth and personal development. And, both are a higher discipline that when learnt add so much to the individual's life. Taekwon-do and university degrees both educate and bring about change – for the better.

It has been said many times, that knowledge is power. It has also been said that knowledge is no weight to carry. This is so true.

Power comes from within as well as from something bigger than ourselves. When these two internal and external sources are harnessed the Taekwon-do student becomes someone who is well on the way to reaching and surpassing their personal milestones.

4.   Keys of Taekwon-do physical fitness

In today's age much emphasis is placed on physical fitness as a key component to being healthy. It's not too hard to dig around in bookshops or on the net to find 'experts' giving their advice on how to reach maximum fitness to accomplish great feats, or how to develop your body in specialist ways to be as fit as humanly possible.

Whilst this is certainly commendable and far better than being lazy, it does at times beg the following questions: "Are such extremes really necessary to live a healthy lifestyle?" or, "Is pushing your body to such lengths sustainable?" And, "Will I still be pushing so hard in five, ten or twenty years' time?"

The answer to these questions is probably no. For while the human body can endure very rigorous training, developing your body to a machine-like fitness level certainly isn't needed for on-going lifestyle fitness and health. Nor, is such an extreme approach within reach for everybody. But, sustainable fitness is.

The great Australian surfer Mark Richards, who is still surfing well into middle age after winning multiple World Surfing Championships as a younger man, knows the importance of ensuring your fitness program is within your capability and continues into your future years as part of a fit and healthy lifestyle.

When commenting about stretching, Mark emphasized the importance of simply doing it at whatever level was achievable no matter how basic. It is not always essential that it's pushed to the limit, just regularly do it as best you can and in a way that suits you.

And, so it is with whatever exercises one does to remain fit. If you can only do five push-ups - then do them. If you can only run 50 metres when you are out jogging - then do it. It's likely that as you become more active you will increase whatever you are doing to an acceptable level that won't break you, but it will keep you fit.

The Chinese approach to exercise is seldom one of great exertion. Tai Chi, walking and shaking of the limbs is hardly a huge physical effort. Each morning across China hundreds of thousands of elderly gather in parks to do no more than these gentle exercises in order to remain physically active in life.

Such an approach will keep you mobile and fit for a very long time. In fact, decades. Becoming fit and maintaining a level of fitness that keeps you freely moving should not burn you out, it should sustain you.

Taekwon-do calls for all its practitioners to be fit. It cannot be otherwise, for it is after all, a physical Martial Art – an art form of fighting and defence. But beyond that essence, it is a lifestyle of fitness as well. Therefore each student needs to find their own sustainable level of fitness. One free from social pressures, gym pressures to be part of the crowd or trends pushing one to extremes they cannot maintain in the long run or may not really need.

Being fit for life can be simple and basic. The real secret is being consistent with whatever one finds as the right on-going level for them so they can continue exercising for the long run without breaking down or exhausting themselves.

There is much value in the basics exercises such as sit-ups, push-ups, swimming, even brisk walking as well as basic stretching. All of which can be done without signing up for expensive programs or engaging personal trainers. Of course, if one does want to push their physical training further through those channels, go ahead. But it's important to remember that the key to life-long fitness and success in living the Taekwon-do life is sustainability.

All of the Taekwon-do patterns aid the student's fitness. They are vigorous and physically demanding. When training and performing these patterns, the student's fitness is enhanced. These patterns are not extreme and when performed time and again, as they will be, they help improve the student's cardiovascular and overall fitness levels. Core strength is built up, as are the arm and leg muscles as all parts of the body are used during training when exercising the stances, kicks and punches etc.

Therefore the TKD patterns with all their various movements assist in building and maintaining the desired long-term fitness level that each student may have in mind – and will need to progress. They are not only vigorous and challenging, but achievable and sustainable. By simply doing Taekwon-do the student is exercising and building fitness and this is available for everyone whatever their individual physical attributes or athletic abilities may be.

5.   The secrets of unleashing your most powerful weapon

Our understanding of the power of positive thinking is not new to us, and now in recent years science and further research have revealed a deeper understanding of the human mind and brain. As the mind and the brain are inexplicitly linked, if indeed, not one and the same thing, what affects one affects the other.

In years past many believed that humans generally used only 10% of their brains. Now with clinical studies and computer imaging clearly showing the brain working, we know that this is not so.

All of us have at our disposal the full use and access to 100% of our brains whilst going about our normal living and daily practices whether we are fully using our brains or not. It is always ready and available for each and every one of us at all times.

Using all of your brain does not mean you are a genius. It is a muscle just like other muscle part of the body. For example, most people generally use all of their legs throughout the day for getting around but that does not make them marathon runners.

However with the brain, there is a slight difference. The brain is made up of two main parts called lobes, which have different functions. One is called the cerebrum and is the seat of creativity and reason. The other is called the cerebellum whose function is to help with co-coordinating human movement.

Each time we think different thoughts, learn different facts, process or challenge our brains to figure something out for ourselves, electromagnetic tracks fire across our brains to the various parts programmed to deal with that particular set of received information.

In short, if we restrict ourselves to thinking the same thoughts over and over again without learning new things or challenging ourselves with mental effort, our brain becomes weak in the areas that are not being used. Just as any other muscle becomes weak when not used or exercised regularly. Similarly, and this is the good news, the brain can be strengthened to perform better, or fired up into maximum 100% use through training, just as any other muscle can.

You may have weak or strong arm muscles, or you may have a weak or strong brain. The secret is to use it, to exercise it. How does one exercise their brain? Not everyone can go to university, for example. True, but everyone can learn and challenge themselves perhaps in their jobs or by undertaking further study of a particular area that they may be interested in. It can be as simple as remembering phone numbers or people's names.

Reading, trying to remember more information or learning something about a topic you knew very little about are basic ways that are very helpful to get started when strengthening the brain. To really power it up into super performance mode, undertaking a higher level of studies of a challenging subject or learning a new language is invaluable.

Lying somewhere in the middle of challenging brain strengthening exercises is Taekwon-do, for there is a set curriculum and body of theory to learn along with a large number of individual body movements to remember when mastering the patterns.

Remembering these particular and varied body movements becomes even more challenging when they have to be repeated in the exact same manner on both sides of the body. What is exercised on one side is then exercised on the other, challenging left and right side brain thinking and coordination so that each side is perfectly reflecting the other.

At first, this precise physical co-ordination may not be easy for some, for it can be mentally challenging and for some students demanding. Some learn it quicker than others. But all students must learn it and in doing so have their brains challenged, exercised and strengthened.

If a brain is being strengthened when learning new Taekwon-do knowledge and complex body movements, as well as the student's determined focus of positive thinking - unstoppable power is freed like a stallion released from captivity to run unhindered into the wild.

It's not only physical power that is unleashed but mental and personal power as well that can then be applied to all areas of a person's life. Taekwon-do is a dynamic power and a very positive way to improve mental health, thinking, reasoning, memory improvement and strengthening the brain's overall performance.

6. The unlimited power of applied thinking

Sadly there is a trait among many people when they come up against a challenge that requires some hard thinking to immediately stop and throw up their hands declaring, "Oh, it's too hard. I couldn't be bothered." Or say, "I quit." In this digital age when computers, smartphones and robots can do a lot of our thinking and problem solving for us, giving up has become too easy.

Another reason for widespread soft thinking is that the digital age has given us so much instant gratification with engaging images, music, computer games, along with the quick and easy 'feel good factor' of social media. We don't have to be too productive or to think of clever ways to amuse ourselves these days as much of it has been already been done for us.

This is of course, wonderful when used correctly – but it's also very harmful in that it can seriously limit mental application as well as hindering the growth of a strong brain and stopping good thinking practices such as memory improvement, critical thinking and problem solving.

Learning to push your thinking to do some hard work when faced with a problem or challenge that is within your mental capacities is a very good habit to form. It strengthens your brain and helps you to grow as a person. Today's modern world challenges us all. It's changing, and it's changing fast. Healthy brains are needed.

Some might wish the fast pace would slow down, and some might want to escape to a dream-like idyllic island in the middle of the Pacific Ocean. Yet, most of us have to equip ourselves as best we can so that we are not just coping or hanging in there, but being productive, smart and succeeding with our lives. That simple success is within reach of us all. And being determined to think when thinking is needed for solutions, ideas, learning and achieving makes for strong mental habits and a healthy brain.

Improving your thinking starts by prioritizing it as an essential part of your life. Set goals – ones that can be attained by trying just that little bit harder than you normally do. Go outside your mental comfort level occasionally. For example, attend a masterclass of some sort, learn a new skill, or a musical instrument, or a new sport, learn to dance, study or go as far to learn a new language.

All of these challenges not only improve the mind but greatly enhance the personal development of the individual. It is wonderful to hear someone say after they have accomplished something that they have strived hard for, "Now I think I walk the earth a little taller." Yes, accomplishment does that for you. And, accomplishment mainly comes about by hard thinking and mental application instead of simply giving up when it becomes tough and demanding.

Throwing your hands up to quit when it gets too hard makes the individual weak and soft. All of us must have a strong resolve or we will accomplish nothing. Once that resolve is in place, there are many sources one can turn to in order to develop more effective and powerful thinking. There are online brain work-outs, books about different subjects other than what we continually read and undertaking various courses such as Taekwon-do which requires mental application as much as a vigorous physical application.

7. Practice propels into power

The golden phrase in real estate is 'location, location, location.' And, so it can be said that when it comes to Taekwon-do, the golden phrase is 'practice, practice, practice.'

It is not unusual for people who are beginning Taekwon-do to feel overwhelmed and somewhat disorientated when first introduced to this Korean Martial Art which consists of a distinct Oriental style of movements and fighting techniques. This is particularly so for Westerners whose culture can be a barrier to identifying with the 'Asianess' of Taekwon-do.

However, once new students start to apply themselves they gradually develop a feel for the art and begin to be aware of what is required to accomplish and to progress.

These ITF Taekwon-do patterns based on historical Korean figures and philosophical thinking consists of various stances, defence blocks, kicks, punches and strikes which blend into a fluid moving pattern that resembles a beautiful dance when performed correctly.

Each pattern is a combination of these many techniques which flow from one to the other with grace, power and an exactness. For Taekwon-do is a precise Martial Art, one that is required to be performed in a very specific way, therefore practice is very important in order to learn that Art just as it is prescribed.

The precision and delivery of these movements are learnt by continual application. In other words, learning through observation - and practice, practice, practice. The term 'muscle memory' is frequently used in Taekwon-do. The instructors will often say, 'Let your muscles become so familiar with what your arms and legs are doing that in time they will perform for you as naturally as a bird flying.'

For indeed birds do fly naturally without thinking of the dangers associated with that huge distance beneath themselves and the earth's hard surface. And humans too, go about their day allowing their muscles to automatically do what they have to do without too much thinking. Legs simply walk without much mental encouragement, as do arms as they get on with their many functions.

It's that level of automatically performing the Taekwon-do movements and patterns that greatly assist the student in mastering the art of Taekwon-do. The patterns have to be executed with a flow that comes out of knowing, out of what has been learnt and from that which has been practiced and deeply embedded in the muscle and mind memories.

The saying, 'Practice makes perfect,' has been mentioned so many times that its truth has almost become blasé. But, this saying is so true. Just as the musician practices, so do dancers, actors or anyone that performs or recites before an audience. No one learns the guitar simply by picking it up. The musician becomes familiar with what is required and then practices and practices. Which, then eventually leads to a level of competence that establishes a confidence to play the instrument well.

And so through continual practicing of the Taekwon-do patterns, the student eventually allows those skills to be so ingrained into their bodies that it enables them to progress, which then enables their confidence to grow.

Confidence comes out of the knowing, and with confidence comes power – and confidence with power is a combination that propels students forward with great impetuous. When Taekwon-do is practiced at this level its true beauty and value as a fighting force starts to shine as an art. As a beautiful art - a beautiful martial art.

After countless hours of practice, practice, practice, Taekwon-do becomes so familiar with the body's memory systems that the student then starts to emerge as a very capable practitioner of the 'once foreign art' of Korea's Taekwon-do. The plant is starting to grow.

That which was once 'foreign' no longer seems that way as it is now an integral part of whom the student is, what they do and what he or she knows.

8. Hidden meanings of ITF Taekwon-do's Tenets

General Choi established five tenets to guide all of ITF Taekwon-do's practitioners. As Taekwon-do is deeply rooted in Asian thinking the practical outworking of these tenets in character traits and habits are often expressed quite differently across cultures. There is however, a core truth to the quality of these tenets that are applicable to all humanity and as such transcends all nationalities and societies.

For example, the Tenets of ITF are inherently noble. Being courteous and possessing integrity are qualities of respect that all honourable people display to others as well as to themselves no matter who they are. So too are the tenets of perseverance and self-control if someone chooses to embody them as an expression of how one lives their life.

For we all know that what we do and how we live not only determines what happens in our own lives but also in the life of others.

Similarly, if someone has an indomitable spirit, which means they won't allow that which is wrong to dominate them nor to be a coward in the face of danger or evil, then that person will easily rise as a champion for justice and what is right – both for themselves and others.

Lions don't back down, nor do champions.

Courtesy is a universal trait. And as such, is found in all cultures around the world. The only difference is in the application according to whoever and how those people are valued within a society. For Asian people, it is important to be courteous towards older people and those with higher status.

In Western societies courtesy is to be shown towards women and those in valued positions of authority such as parents, teachers and dignitaries. Not necessarily hierarchal.

However the universal application of courtesy, and this is certainly in line with Taekwon-do culture, is to be shown to all peoples no matter what their position or status may be.

At the root of treating all people with courtesy is an acknowledgement of the international brotherhood of all peoples. After all we are one humanity, and Taekwon-do recognizes this. It certainly isn't one step too far to state that if everyone showed courtesy to each other the world would be a far better place and probably without wars.

Just as a tamed tiger can be the most gentlest of animals, so can a fighting force like Taekwon-do be an instrument for international peace.

Integrity is, sadly, almost a lost quality in this modern age. Integrity means having an honesty and a sincerity which has often been referred to as a healthy wholeness – and that is a wonderful description.

People who have integrity can be trusted and relied upon. Their word is as good as their bond. Those with integrity carry that quality into all they do and into their interactions with other people. This is also showing respect as well as promoting peaceful living.

Perseverance is a quality that has wider understanding in modern living as people have become more goal-orientated. Not always to develop improved personal character, but often to let their accomplishments aid their accumulation of finances and the status tagged along with monetary gains.

This is not the purpose of Taekwon-do in promoting perseverance. TKD perseverance is encouraged so the student may never quit striving towards improving and accomplishing their goals.

Being able to control one's self is sometimes harder than climbing Mt Everest. Possessing self-control starts with being honest with yourself about your strengths and weaknesses. Particularly weakness – which is not always easy for us to face up to. After all, who enjoys having their faults pointed out to them? But, it has to be done.

It has been said that in order to conquer the world, one must first conquer themselves. Knowing what inhibits you from progressing is as important as knowing what you are good at. And, there can be no meaningful self-control without that knowledge.

Most everyone has faced danger at some point in their lives. Be it from a mishap or from someone else's threatening behavior. Most have faced fear as well and some people at one point or another have backed down when they shouldn't have. Being a person of indomitable spirit means that you are no longer willing to be one who backs down, or perhaps one that never did. It doesn't mean being fearless, but having an indomitable spirit means that such a person will not let fear rule them when it's time to stand up and be counted.

These tenets are a call for all people to be as one in a universal brotherhood. Although Taekwon-do is a fighting martial art, it holds as its core an intention for a harmonious and a peaceful world - and that is Taekwon-do's hidden gift to all humanity.

9. The hidden strengths of ITF Taekwon-do's Oath

Saying an oath, or giving an oath before others or to an institution, is not to be done lightly. It's a declaration of loyalty according to mutual understanding and a commitment to abide by that loyalty. An oath when once given, means that the person declaring it can therefore be relied upon and trusted as a person to faithfully keep the words that he, or she, has spoken.

Taekwon-do has an oath that each student is asked to pledge adherence to. This oath does not exist simply for the sake of loyalty, but that the student who agrees to it may be guided by clear principles to be incorporated into their lives in order to become a person of worthwhile character.

There is an unbreakable truth embodied within Taekwon-do. TKD is like a pillar that one can rely on or a well of life-giving water to draw from when needed. For just as bamboo is strong and at times unbreakable, so too is Taekwon-do. Therefore by following the ITF Oath students take on character traits of that oath which then begins to shape their lives.

As Taekwon-do imparts its dynamics to its students, the students learn and gain much. They grow into people who are empowered with skills, knowledge, maturity and strength. Particularly by building the tenets, practices and truths of Taekwon-do into their characters and allowing these truths to then shape who they will become with distinction.

Yes, Taekwon-do as a martial art is a form of fighting, and yes General Choi Hong Hi taught it to the soldiers of the Korean Army, but it is much more than that. It is a way of living. A way to become a true warrior - a warrior of life and not one merely limited to the military or to fighting.

A student does not pledge to Taekwon-do's Oath so as to become a fighter, but to be a reliable and trustworthy citizen of the world. Specifically, a peaceful citizen. The strength that Taekwon-do gives you must never be used for your own ego, gain or to cause suffering to others.

The world needs champions. Not just because of the big things that are wrong in the world like wars and poverty but also on the everyday level. The small boy in the neighborhood needs a champion, the bullied kid at school needs a champion, the softer person who is picked on at work needs one and so does the battered woman who suffers behind closed doors.

The Taekwon-do Oath asks all students to be champions wherever they are and in whatever capacity whenever they are needed.

Most of the conflicts and injustices in the world today are due to many people in high places of government and influence who fed their egos and furthered their own selfish plans at the expense of others.

The Taekwon-do student is to be the very opposite as they pledge the Taekwon-do Oath towards making the world a more peaceful place. The TKD student builds peace in the home, the family, their relationships, at work and in all that they do.

10. Why embracing Korean aids Taekwon-do

Challenging oneself to step outside the familiar or your 'comfort zone,' is at times to be encouraged. For not only does it expand an individual's life experience for growth and knowledge, it also opens up avenues for creativity.

If there had not been thinkers who took time out to dream, to explore and to push themselves past what they were comfortable with mankind would not have walked on the moon, invented refrigerators or written masterpieces ... or drawn comics!

Nor would have General Choi Hong Hi conceived a martial art whose quality of lifestyle he saw as a gift to the world. ITF Taekwon-do was born of a large vision. And as such, challenges its practitioners to also be big thinkers.

Very few of us will think of the next 'big thing,' but we certainly can step a little outside our 'feel-good' safe boundaries once and a while to embrace or learn something that challenges us. It's not insisted upon in all Dojongs, however some do mandate that each student learns a basic level of the Korean language. For example counting to ten in Korean:

One – Hana
Two – Dool
Three – Set
Four – Net
Five – Dasot
Six – Yasot
Seven – Ilgop

Eight – Yodul
Nine – Ahop
Ten – Yol

It's a big commitment to learn words from another language. Their foreign sounds and grammar are not always easy to master. One of the wonderful benefits however, is that in the process of learning, the student is exposed to another culture.

As Korean is an ancient (one of the oldest in the world) exotic and deeply Asian culture, it has much to offer those who allow some of its characteristics into their lives. Becoming a little bit 'Korean' is a good thing to do.

It is enriching, or in the case of some students, an experience that takes them to a place where they find themselves. Or at least find some aspects of another society that helps formulate their individual identity and growth.

There are many benefits to learning as much as you can of another culture and its language. It expands personal horizons, builds an understanding of others and prepares you mentally to appreciate and learn something of the foreign culture you are identifying with.

Many people who learn a foreign language often travel to that country and forge life-long friends there. Or, what better way to ensure your travel to the country of choice is that much richer due to you learning their language? It's a great way to fully appreciate all you see and experience when visiting.

It is quite common for those Taekwon-do students who have learnt some of the Korean language and who have travelled to that land to say they now feel more attached to all that Taekwon-do represents. Learning some Korean is another generous way for 'foreigners' to show appreciation and respect to General Choi Hong Hi, to his homeland and to all that Taekwon-do has given us.

Taekwon-do is not just another sport or way of fighting, it is a lifestyle designed for the whole person. Yes it is international, but it is essentially Korean, which when fully infused into each student's life, deepens that life with knowledge and a sense of enrichment.

11. The significance of colour belts

The use of colours in symbolism and meaning is very common in most cultures. Their purposes often vary according to different functions as well as the contextual importance of that colour's meaning to that particular country and way of life.

Red means revolution in countries that have undergone social upheaval, while in China red not only means revolution but is widely used to represent luck. Whereas in Western countries red means danger.

Colour meanings can be very important, which may be for fun or for a simple practical reason. Such as red for stop and green for go.

Indeed the list is endless and fascinating.

Purple means royalty and wisdom. It can also represent a personality type indicating sensitivity and compassion.

Green is said to be the colour of life representing nature. It is also associated with envy.

Yellow is a representation of sunshine and warmth, while psychologically it is the colour of an effective communicator.

Brown is an interesting colour as some people consider it dull, while for others it means dependability and health.

The list does go on and on. No doubt the reader could add quite a few other examples themselves.

In Taekwon-do colours also have important meanings. They represent the life of the student and his/her's relationship with the earth's nurturing powers and the student's progression through Taekwon-do as well as progressing through life.

When the full significance of each of these colours is studied in sequence an insight can be gained into the mind of General Choi. Quite clearly he understood that a person's life in Taekwon-do was to do with development and maturity. Or perhaps in more simple terms, growing into your own unique self and fulfilling your potential. It certainly does not mean going through life merely to have fun and to accumulate as much money as you possibly can. This is far too limiting.

Material comfort is very desirable, but when it is out of balance and becomes the most important focus it's not wealth at all but a warping of the true self, and sometimes imprisonment. Taekwon-do seeks to do the opposite, which is to help the individual successfully grow and be free of life's restricting snares.

The Taekwon-do life is meaningful in that the sequential steps of accomplishment assist in the growth of the individual person. Taekwon-do's use of colours signifies this growth as the students pass each particular level moving forward. Each colour is a progressive step upwards to a higher level and indicates achievement.

The obtaining of each colour belt is therefore one step further to mastering the art as well as passing significant milestones of personal development throughout the student's Taekwon-do journey.

12. Interpreting the hidden meanings in ITF Taekwon-do's patterns

Korea is one of the oldest cultures on Earth, commonly believed to be approximately five thousand years old. Surprisingly, for a country that has given the world a fighting martial art, Korea does not have a history of invading another country. Yes, it has been involved in wars but never as the aggressor.

Five thousand years is a long time to live in peace with your neighbours, something that the rest of the world could do well to emulate. And, five thousand years is a long time to accumulate a deep rich history, which is honoured in Taekwon-do.

The nine patterns of ITF Taekwon-do that students master from white belt to black have been given names that reflect a deep respect for key historical figures drawn from Korea's past.

With the exception of the first pattern which is named appropriately after heaven and earth emphasizing the beginning of creation, all the patterns are named after great men and one outstanding youth group.

Each of these significant figures has played a pivotal role in Korea's history. They founded the nation, shaped its education, as well as contributing to its philosophical and spiritual depth that has made Korea the nation that it is today.

These men are rightly considered to be the fathers of the nation as they exemplify the very best qualities in fatherhood of fostering and implementing a vision. They were men who looked ahead to the coming generations to create a nation home that would last long into the future. True fatherhood means nurturing and providing an environment where the family or nation can grow, live in peace and happiness and be prosperous.

The men honoured in Taekwon-do accomplished exactly that. They were indeed giants on whose shoulders Korea, and us as Taekwon-do's students (no matter our nationality), stand.

It is deeply rooted in Korea's Confucian society to highly value filial love. That is to say, love and respect of parents and ancestors. Whilst honouring these particular men fulfils that duty there is also an abiding sense that the nation's fathers are held in genuine reverence as much as being honoured merely out of compulsion.

That IFT Taekwon-do chose to name its patterns, which are at the very heart of its dynamic essence, after these founding figures, indicates the deep noble nature of Taekwon-do itself. For Taekwon-do, stated in simple terms, doesn't primarily teach you to fight, it teaches you to live out the very best qualities of nobility.

TKD teaches you to follow in the footsteps of these men of vision and big spirit. If you are a father, how big is your vision? Is it three or four generations deep? Indeed, is it to father an entire nation? Or to guide an existing one? How many fathers do that? Very few, but fathering with the best of your heart and ability towards one child or two, or whatever number you might have in your family is just as needed as great leaders of nations. A noble heart really does start at home and should first be practiced right there.

Do you have a call that you feel is a destiny for your life, do you have a duty or are you a parent? How will you go about performing these responsibilities in your life? Will you follow in the footsteps of great men lifting up your eyes to accomplish something much greater for the benefits of others?

Founding fathers of nations may not be needed in these modern times, but men and women who draw from their example to live out their lives to the best of their abilities certainly are.

Everyday fathers, mothers, and community leaders have the lives of these honoured Korean fathers whose footsteps are clearly marked on the path of life, for us to follow. And, as students of Taekwon-do it is our calling and duty to do so.

13. How to lay your foundation for fighting

As a martial art Taekwon-do has at its core a style of fighting that is quite aggressive.

Tae means foot or to strike with the feet. Kwon means hand or to strike with the hand. Do means discipline, art, or way. Hence Taekwon-do (foot-hand-way) literally means the art of the feet and the hands or the art of kicking and punching.

To use your hands and feet effectively, the Taekwon-do fighter must be in the correct stance for each attack so he, or she, is able to strike with the maximum force. For each attack, as with each defensive block, Taekwon-do has a specific stance designed to aid the fighter.

These stances must be learnt as they are the foundation for all that the student uses throughout their Taekwon-do life as an active fighter.

The stances that the novice learns with the first pattern are the same one that masters use well into their Black Belt life as their Taekwon-do skills deepen.

The stances aid him or her to be the quickest, the most powerful and to defend as best as possible when repelling or minimizing their opponent's attack.

Fundamentally the stances are designed so the fighter is on a rock solid base. Or to put it another way, it's like gripping the earth with the soles of your feet so you are not easily pushed around. As most of Taekwon-do is practiced bare-footed, it's very easy to visualize your feet doing just that. And, it works.

Yes, the stances are very exact and must be strictly mastered, but by using your mind to aid in imagining you are joined to the earth with your stance helps foster a feeling of added strength to the fighter.

And, from that rock-solid foundation balance and flexibility are easily drawn upon when needed to strike like a cat or to block like a bull.

Learning the stances and fine tuning them through continual practice is learnt in conjunction with using ITF Taekwon-do's sine wave movement that springs out of the stances. The sine wave is the motion of bending your knees in order to lower your body in the stance you are using and as the student's body then rises into the attack, extra power is released into the punch or strike.

Therefore the sine wave's power can only be fully released in attack if the student's stance is correct.

Stances are to be studied, mastered and visualized so an immovable foundation is laid. A foundation that will aid the student to build solid Taekwon-do fighting skills that will serve him, or her, right throughout their long and rich Taekwon-do life.

14. Unlocking the dynamic of punching

The Korean word Kwon means hand, or to strike with the hand - to punch. Although Taekwon-do is a martial art that uses both hands and feet to attack, punching is a very important part of its striking power and is at the heart of its fighting style.

Taekwon-do teaches its students to spar off against their opponents with a light-footed skip so they are able to size up their opponent and attack quickly from any angle. This ensures the opponent doesn't know what might be launched at them next.

Muhammad Ali's famous quote to 'Float like a butterfly, sting like a bee' sums it up very well. As does Bruce Lee's fighting style which was described as a cat treading softly in order to strike very quickly.

When Taekwon-do fighters unleash their punches from the correct stance backed with the extra force coming out of the sine wave rise, their punches becomes a powerful means of attack.

It's vital to move around, change the lead hand and vary the punches. The fighter's arms are to be held lightly in defense but used like steel pistons when lashing out.

Taekwon-do fighters use a number of leads to punch from various angles. And, when the appropriate punch is thrown according to the opponent's exposed weakness, the opponent will only see it coming micro seconds before the punch hits its mark.

Being ready to punch, knowing how to punch and striking with the correct punch at the right time are all taught in Taekwon-do's syllabus. This is so that the hours of practice drilled into the student gives he, or she, an intuitive feel about how to punch as if by second nature.

These different punches are designed to be delivered with maximum force combining technique and utilizing the natural flow of the human body. When this is understood by the student and springs forth in fighting from the mind infused with Taekwon-do philosophy, the fighter's punches become a prime method of attack that makes him or her very hard to defeat.

Therefore Taekwon-do's punches do not rely solely on muscle power. To punch using only your own strength is too limiting. It reduces the contest to a shoot-out between who is the strongest. With Taekwon-do, strength is only one of the components of punching. And, with a great variety of punches used to attack this gives the

Taekwon-do fighter, no matter their size, an advantage or at least helps level the playing field.

Along with punches, there is a full range of strikes and thrusts that have been developed in order to make full use of the hand as a striking weapon. These are clever and very effective, arming the fighter with a variety of options when using the hands in attack.

Effective punching Taekwon-do style is fluid, dynamic and when unleashed in fighting assists in making smart and powerful fighters.

15. The importance of Taekwon-do kicking

The Korean word Tae means foot, specifically when the foot is used as a weapon to destroy. This definition alone gives some indication as to the force of Taekwon-do's kicking style and its numerous striking abilities.

Kicking is very important in Taekwon-do as a martial art. It is exact, it has a number of variations in delivery and when unleashed correctly can prove to be the winning edge needed in sparring and fighting. Having a well-aimed foot flying at your chest or face with full force is very formidable and as such is a major strike weapon that quickly unsettles opponents.

Indeed, it is not uncommon for a well-timed kick to take out an opponent or to be the telling blow that hands the winning bout or title to a fighter. All of the very best Taekwon-do warriors have great kicking abilities.

The good news is, as in all things Taekwon-do, every student can master these techniques and employ them to full use no matter what level of overall competency the student may have. For Taekwon-do can be practiced by all peoples of all shapes and sizes and with all levels of ability.

As long as the kicks are technically sound it is not essential that their striking range and power matches that of someone who has the ability to kick higher and faster. Nor will a limited strike range mean that the kick will be delivered with reduced force.

A well-executed kick landed cleanly at the right time on any part of an opponent's body can cause a lot of damage and go a long way to disarming the opponent or enemy's attack.

Taekwon-do kicks are launched from the front, the side, the back and while the student is in the air using both or either one of the legs. The kicks are also aimed at every part of the opponent's body from the head to the feet. General Choi gave a lot of thought to his Taekwon-do kicking style as he knew the capabilities of the human body as well as its vulnerable striking points.

With his Oriental mind understanding the importance of working with the body's natural flow and harnessing the energy of movement, means that General Choi's Taekwon-do kicking techniques draw on much more than simply kicking out blindly. They draw on natural laws of energy flow and what the body can do effortlessly in unison with that universal power.

This is one of the great strengths of Taekwon do. It works with nature and the individuality of each practitioner's body and abilities. That is also one of the reasons why Taekwon-do's kicking is so powerful and when well executed can render an opponent ineffective or a defeated foe.

The kicks of Taekwon-do contribute a great deal to the beauty of it as a martial art. The kicks are delivered with precision, force and at the right time. As they flow out of correct positioning with the rhythm of Taekwon-do's fighting style, their free-flowing force can be an awesome sight of beauty as well as a fearsome one.

16. The dynamic of the Taekwon-do fighter

It was once suggested that certain masters of martial arts had to register their hands as lethal weapons. In reality, that was most likely no more than an urban myth doing the rounds for a lark.
Still, like a lot of things that are spoken about in a light-hearted manner, there is sometimes a grain of truth in it. Taekwon-do certainly trains it students to be powerful fighters but it definitely doesn't train them to be unnecessarily aggressive and threatening in any form whatsoever. All students are taught restraint and respect.

They do not become reckless, dangerous warriors. Yes, they certainly become fighters but under strict self-discipline and adherence to Taekwon-do's code of becoming quality people and to build a more peaceful world. They are probably best described as becoming 'warriors of life.'

Taekwon-do fighters become highly-trained martial art practitioners who can also use their skills for health, fitness, self-esteem, self-defense and cultivation of the mind. That's an impressive set of ideals and a very long way from training people who may have to register their hands as lethal weapons. Indeed, it's not an exaggeration to state that if everyone in the world practiced Taekwon-do correctly the world would be a far better place – and without wars.

Taekwon-do does not teach senseless violence for its own sake nor to release wild, dangerous egos onto the street to cause trouble. That is the very opposite to the core philosophy of this martial art which has deep roots in a rich holistic Asian culture where uncalled-for violence is not acceptable.

Korea which has enabled its culture to flourish on the teachings of Confucius, the Buddha and Taoism seeks harmony between all the forces that nature releases, recognizing that they do not oppose each other but co-exist as one. Indeed, the other keeps its opposite alert and as a reminder not to slip into compliancy believing only in its own essence. Taekwon-do springs from this culture of understanding and tolerance.

By accepting the 'other' in whatever form one may find it, is a far cry from breeding aggression. This does not mean you have to like everything and everybody but does mean you do not oppose it with force or hate. Therefore enemies and unwarranted violence are not created by someone who may be tempted to forcefully oppose what they cannot accept or find abhorrent. All that one might dislike or cannot accept is to be dealt with according to Taekwon-do thought and training.

Taekwon-do produces people who Bruce Lee described as being soft but do not yield - firm but not hard.

It is also taught in Korea, as it is throughout much of Asia, to honour and respect elders. These two attributes foster dignity and nobility which are characteristics of people whose contribution to life is of considerable value. As well as being people who do not turn away from all that is good and correct.

Taekwon-do is to be harnessed and used in its right manner so that its practitioners become world citizens that are marked with distinction. And, it is a force for light that takes its place in the world to stand against whatever darkness may be found.

The Taekwon-do fighter does indeed have sharpened fighting skills that enable him, or her to be strong in combat. However, the application of these skills is far wider than simply fighting for its own sake as they are designed primarily to be a force of strength, fitness, wholeness and nobility.

17. Becoming and being a Black Belt

For many people their Taekwon-do journey ends when they attain their black belt, while for others it is only the completion of the first stage with a long path still ahead of them.

Either way, their individual journey that started with that one first step has reached a significant milestone. Becoming a Black Belt is a considerable achievement and all who attain that status are to be congratulated, for it was not won easily or cheaply. Years of dedicated training and discipline were devoted to winning that goal.

It has been written that only one in ten thousand who start a martial art will go on to become a Black Belt. That is not very good odds, so clearly those that do so have achieved a very significant personal goal that few others will never reach.

It is a long journey with challenges and victories accompanied with many highs and lows along the way just as any journey of significance is. And, it can be lonely at times too. Students train and learn with others but they also spend many hours practicing alone. However one may choose to train, essentially any accomplishments in Taekwon-do are individual ones. The hardships and the triumphs are yours and yours alone, even when shared with your club and instructors.

But what does it mean to become a Black Belt? Although many Black Belts walk amongst us, they are not easy to spot at first glance. They certainly do not walk around looking like dangerous people. However, many do possess something of a sterling nature that is distinctively noticeable once you are able to observe how they conduct their everyday affairs.

For they have learnt and become something of Taekwon-do themselves and as such exhibit fine character qualities such as dependability, trustworthiness, 'stickability' and very often leadership traits. Many of them are successful in their own quiet way wherever they may work and do business.

It is not unusual for Black Belt people to be effective achievers in most areas of their lives, for that which they have acquired along the way of their Taekwon-do journey serves them very well in everyday living. They are flexible but strong, patient but quick, know how to hurry but do so slowly and are determined to proceed further with their life's journey while being content to be still learning. These qualities and skills are life skills, not merely Taekwon-do ones alone.

Just as importantly 'Black Belters' are stewards. Stewards of what they have acquired and of shouldering the responsibility of being an honourable world citizen. Many of them have come from non-Asian countries but having been infused so deeply into Taekwon-do they now carry something of the Orient within themselves. They have become international people.

As Taekwon-do is practiced worldwide Black Belt people can be found in many nations forging them all into a unique brotherhood that stretches across borders, gender, race, religion, and age. And as such, they now possess a larger worldview and share Taekwon-do's global identity, lifestyle and duty.

They might have thought they were only training towards their Black Belt when they first started their Taekwon-do journey, but now that they have acquired it they have become a 'Black Belt citizen.' They are an example for all those who follow them and to all with whom they interact and live with.

The Taekwon-do Black Belt is a brotherhood shared through their common Taekwon-do oath, tenets, values and accomplishments which have led them all towards the same finish line. And, there they stand, just as General Choi envisioned, students who have become all that Taekwon-do has to offer and now they must use it to further peace, be a champion against injustice and work towards building a better world.

For Taekwon-do not only builds a better world, it also builds better people.

*   *   *

Train, study and enjoy your Taekwon-Do journey.